MW00786867

FUSION

CHILDREN'S MINISTRY
BOOK ONE: THEOLOGY, LEADERSHIP, CULTURE

Created by the Northwest Ministry Network:
Brent Colby, Lauren Beach, Dave M. Cameron, Craig Geis,
Dorene Heeter, Sam Korslund, Dan Metteer, Chantel Rohr,
Kate Thaete, and Joshua R. Ziefle

Copyright © 2015 by the Northwest Ministry Network

All rights reserved.

Northwest Ministry Network

35131 SE Douglas St. #200

Snoqualmie WA 98065

www.nwministry.com

Scriptures marked ESV taken from *The Holy Bible, English Standard Version,*
copyright © 2001 by Crossway Bibles, a publishing ministry of Good News
Publishers.

Scriptures marked NASB taken from the *New American Standard Bible®,* Copyright
© 1960, 1962, 1963, 1968, 1971, 1972, 1973, 1975, 1977, 1995 by The
Lockman Foundation. Used by permission.

Scriptures marked NIV taken from the *Holy Bible, New International Version®,*
NIV® Copyright © 1973, 1978, 1984, 2011 by Biblica, Inc.® Used by
permission. All rights reserved worldwide.

Scriptures marked NLT taken from the *Holy Bible, New Living Translation,* copyright
© 1996. Used by permission of Tyndale House Publishers, Inc., Wheaton,
Illinois 60189. All Rights reserved.

To Kevin:

This book is the fruit of your loins—we mean labor.

Thank you for investing into us so that we can invest into others.

CONTENTS

INTRODUCTION

0.0 - THE BIG IDEA
Brent Colby

WHY WE WROTE THIS BOOK

I work with some of the greatest children's pastors in the world. My role as a ministry director allows me to connect with a variety of leaders, teachers, and preachers, and I have found that the amount of talent surging through local church is amazing. These individuals serve in ministries that are big and small, communities that are urban and rural, and with budgets that are rich and poor. Each is differentw each is talented. These men and women have found ways to lead with their gifts and are having a great impact on their churches and communities

When I hear their stories, I get excited about what God is doing, because their testimonies encourage me and challenge me to do better. Something special happens when we team up and share ideas. Daniel J. Levi believes that "team members help and learn from one another. Not only does the team perform better, but so do most of the individual members."[1] We learn, we adopt, and we become better together. God doesn't intend for us to serve him as lone rangers. We read that, "two are better than one,"[2] that "iron sharpens iron,"[3] and that "each has received a gift to serve the other."[4] No individual has figured out the best way to "do ministry," and I believe there is no such thing. Instead, God gives each of us insight and a unique way of contributing to the Church at large.[5] We are different and we serve different functions in the "body of Christ."[6] Some of us are hands while others are feet, and we need each other to fulfill Christ's vision for the Church. We have greater influence together than we could ever have alone.

Fusion happens when two or more things collide to form a single object.[7] Scientists study nuclear fusion to understand expressions of incredible power. This book is also about fusion. The power unleashed when these ideas combine can't be stopped by any force on earth. God's truth is being revealed to us so that we might form a greater, more complete vision of children's ministry today. We have collected a series of big ideas for you to think about. Each of them exists as a variable in a large equation. Throw them together and allow your views of ministry to get smacked around a bit. Embrace that collision and see how the Holy Spirit will empower you to tell people about Jesus in a new way.[8]

We want to provoke a conversation. The following pages represent a series of key ideas surrounding children and the Church. This is not a conclusive guide; if you're looking for all of the answers, then this is the wrong place. Our goal is to have you think and discuss the ways in which you approach ministry to kids. Read it alone or read it with a team. Questions have been placed at the end of each chapter to help you work through the concepts.

How It Came Together

This book was born at a meeting with ten pastors and a blank sheet of paper. We started writing down *big ideas about children's ministry*. The list was short at first; we covered basics like prayer, biblical literacy, and worship. Before long the list covered topics such as brain plasticity, psychosocial group dynamics, and digital learning environments. We ended with sixty-four *big ideas* and set out to categorize them.

Many hours later we emerged with some themes. Today these themes include theology, leadership, environment, family, science, strategy, history, culture, and pastoral care. Our goal is to discuss each of these categories in turn in this book. Are there more categories? Sure. Where are subjects like discipleship, pastoral care, and volunteers? They are in here; we chose to discuss those as subsets of other categories. Understand that there are many ways to organize this work but, at the end of the day, we had to pick one. So this is it.

Who Wrote It

The authors are pastors with varied backgrounds. Some have PhDs, others GEDs; some work in small farming communities, others in major universities. I think one is left-handed. They are smart and, with a few exceptions, good-looking.[9] The diverse nature of the group is an asset. Our goal is to share thoughts from people who have something to say. There is value for you to hear from different voices off the beaten path. Just as Steven Johnson argues when describing the origin of good ideas, "The trick to having good ideas is not to sit around in glorious isolation and try to think big thoughts. The trick is to get more parts on the table."[10] Our gift to you is lots of parts. But these contributions are not unproven, every one of these leaders has been successful and wants to share with you. They have something to offer, if you are willing to take it.

Our team reminds me of a stained glass window. Imagine small pieces of glass that are different shapes and colors, fixed together with a framework of leading but lacking symmetry or pattern. Anyone with a close-up view would say that the window is not beautiful, not a complete picture of anything. But when you step back and see the work at large, you gain a sense of scope, of completeness. The Church has used stained glass to share the story of Christ with generations. These works inspire awe and humility. And each work is never made with anything more than odd-shaped pieces of glass stuck together. This project is that.

Framework Makes the Game Work

You know what they say: "Framework makes the game work." Actually, no one says that—but they should! Understanding how something is built provides great insight into that thing. When it comes to books,

Mortimer J. Adler says that, "Every book has a skeleton hidden between its boards. Your job is to find it."[11] Let me save you some time and explain how we have organized the *Fusion Children's Ministry* series.

We are dealing with no fewer than twenty-seven ideas, spread out over nine parts, in three different books. You're almost done with the introduction of book one . . . so you haven't really started yet. This book (book one) addresses *theology, leadership,* and *environment* as they relate to children's ministry. Books two and three will pick up with the rest of the aforementioned themes. We have designed the *Fusion Children's Ministry* series to be an iterative work, which means we plan to add to this text in the future.

CLICK CLICK

Bang! Let's get started. You are doing some of the most important work the Church has ever done. I pray that this book will be encouraging and challenging for you, and that it will start discussions about children's ministry in your own church.

PART ONE: THEOLOGY

Theology is concerned with the nature of God and religious belief. It is an important place to start when discussing any function of the Church, including children's ministry. Discovering your leadership style, communication strategy, or stage design is hopeless without a firm foundation in Scripture. We must understand the elements that relate to *why* we do children's ministry, and not just *how.*

Dr. Joshua R. Ziefle is going to discuss "The Biblical Nature of Discipleship" and reveal what the Bible says about ministry to kids. Kate will broach the subject of "Kids Becoming Christian." I hope you dig deeply into this one; it is critical that we clearly describe the process of salvation to kids. Finally, David M. Cameron is going to examine "The Big Deal About Kids and Worship." He breaks down some bad theology in Christmas music so prepare your heart for that. You'll never sing "Away in a Manger" the same way again.

1.1 - THE BIBLICAL NATURE OF DISCIPLESHIP
Joshua R. Ziefle

INTRODUCTION

Christians are truly people of the Book. We are encouraged to read it regularly, meditate upon its precepts, and gather weekly to reflect on its call as we walk the life of faith. It is a sure and steady guide that points to the Word of God—Jesus—and we are blessed to live in a world where the Bible is so readily available.

It goes without saying that the Bible covers a lot of ground in its sixtyF six books. Love, hate, war, peace, salvation, and damnation: it's all there. Some themes are repeated again and again throughout the story of God, while others appear much less frequently, such as the topic of children.

Though it may not be popular to write this in a book on children's ministry, I'll be honest: Kids are *not* one of the predominant themes of Scripture. Compared to other ideas such as grace, sin, obedience, and spiritual gifts, childhood gets relatively little attention. Even so, the presence of children in the pages of the Bible reminds us of some foundational truths which, while not always overt, have important implications for the discipleship of the children under our care.

This chapter will identify five biblical themes: blessing, training, obedience, transience, and ubiquity. Each of these represents an aspect of the Scripture's reflections on children. While initially not all of them seem to have direct impact upon ministry to kids, I believe they are valuable ideas upon which we should reflect. After we look at such biblical themes, key principles will be discerned that should have an impact upon the way we interact with children as we help them walk down the road of discipleship.

THE BIBLE ON CHILDHOOD

The first and perhaps most foundational theme related to children in the Bible is that they are a *blessing*. As the source of new life, the perpetuation of the human lineage, and the growth of the family, children represent a deep joy within the Scripture. As we read in Psalm 127:3, "Children are a heritage from the Lord, offspring a reward from him."[12] Of such value is this emerging generation that the psalmist goes on to tell us that "blessed is the man whose quiver is full of them."[13]

If we think about the promises to Abraham, the protection of Moses in the reeds, the deep sorrow at Herod's murder of the innocents, combined with the great joy at the coming of Christ, the Bible is clear: children are a great gift to us. Those of us who work with them on a regular basis, including parents, know this full well. Though there are tough seasons mixed in with more joyous ones, the blessedness of new life is a biblical affirmation that is confirmed regularly in our lives.

A second biblical theme related to childhood is somewhat different. We shift our attention from how we should view children to how they are supposed to respond to adults. *Obedience* is the key word, and the Bible shows children how to honor their parents.. In the New Testament, Paul writes plainly: "Children, obey your parents in the Lord, for this is right."[14] The connection between parental obedience and further biblical truth is made as he links it to the Fifth Commandment: "Honor your father and your mother, so that you may live long in the land the Lord your God is giving you."[15]

Though such commands are linked together with the family unit, the fact that they are rooted in the Ten Commandments and the Law itself implies that obedience is not just about honoring father and mother, but about following after God himself. Such an imperative is not only for children to consider but for all those who encounter the Scripture.

I realize, of course, that the Christian is saved by grace and not works and that the idea of behavior modification for its own sake is (rightfully) somewhat discredited in children's and youth ministry.[16] This does not negate the fact that there are a host of actions to which we and all believers are called. While such actions are meant to flow out of a relationship with God and not simply to be performed for their own sake, the stance of obedience to God and others is vital. Those serving in children's ministry are, together with parents, at the "front lines" of communicating the importance of obedience.

A third biblical theme flows from the second: *training*. When we are born we know and are able to do very little. As we grow and develop over time, our ability to understand and interact with our world increases. The long story of human history has shown these emerging abilities to be a mixed bag. In all of us the same potential for obedience and service sits uncomfortably next to the opportunity for sin and destruction. For those discipling children, helping them towards obedience through training is important.

The Book of Proverbs majors on training: "Start children off on the way they should go, and even when they are old they will not turn from it."[17] Catchy and well worth reflecting upon, such an idea has deep roots in the biblical tradition. I think here of the famous passage in Deuteronomy where the Israelites are called to raise up following generations in the ways of the Lord:

These commandments that I give you today are to be on your hearts. Impress them on your children. Talk about them when you sit at home and when you walk along the road, when you lie down and when you get up. Tie them as symbols on your hands and bind them on your foreheads. Write them on the door frames of your houses and on your gates.[18]

The Bible is clear on the value of God's words and living in the light of His truth. The next generation—our children—need to know that these are not merely abstract concepts, but rather transformational realities. They need to be trained with regard to the story of God, the life of faith, and their deep place within it. As if this were not important enough in its own right, the fact that other forces will train our children if we do not should serve as a clear reminder.

The final two biblical themes I will identify are not imperatives as much as they are reminders. The fourth, for instance, has to do with the *transience* of childhood. Simply stated, children grow up. The Bible uses such an obvious truth to great effect. First Peter 2:2–3 borrows from the metaphor of infancy to command believers to, "like newborn babies, crave pure spiritual milk, so that by it you may grow up in your salvation, now that you have tasted that the Lord is good." Paul uses a similar metaphor when he writes to "mere infants in Christ" whom he gave "milk, not solid food, for [they] were not yet ready for it."[19] Those of us discipling believers of any age should be convicted and edified by such words, but such ideas take on added importance when working with those who are closer to actual infancy.

The Bible sees the life of discipleship to be one of progress and development, much like the growth of a child who moves through various stages on his or her journey to adulthood. Childhood is temporary. It is transient. So too should be our spiritual infancy. There are appropriate levels and stages for children in their walk with God, but this level of faith can never be static and must always be progressing.

The fifth and final theme we will discuss is *ubiquity*. As defined by Merriam Webster, ubiquity means: "presence everywhere or in many places especially simultaneously."[20] At the most obvious level this simply means that childhood is an ever-present reality. With the exception of Eden, children have been present throughout the human and biblical story. In every time and place, even when not directly mentioned, they are there. The next generation has always been rising, even as in its growth and development they have been setting the stage for the one to come.

The ubiquity of childhood is about something much deeper than just numbers. Childhood, the Bible says, should not simply be a demographic fact of human existence, but something alive in each of us. Inasmuch as childhood is transient and we all are called to "grow up," there is a part of the innocence of youth that must never leave us. Some of this can be seen as John addresses believers: "And now, dear children, continue in him, so that when he appears we may be confident and unashamed before him at his coming. If you know that he is righteous, you know that everyone who does what is right has been born of him."[21] In a grandfatherly way, John looks at his flock and simply calls them children, not in a demeaning fashion and not, I think, implying that their faith is wholly immature. He is using the term "children" respectfully and lovingly.

John's words are reminiscent of what Jesus said to his disciples in Matthew 18:3–4 (NIV): "Truly I tell you, unless you change and become like little children, you will never enter the kingdom of heaven. Therefore, whoever takes the lowly position of this child is the greatest in the kingdom of heaven." The ubiquity of childhood is something that needs to be a part of each believer's life. The call to be a child is not a call toward immaturity or ignorance, but toward faith and trust. The way in which a child embraces Jesus Christ ought to be the way we embrace. A child—especially the youngest among us—has no recourse but to trust and depend on others. This lesson is undeniable, and must be put into practice in our lives. The ubiquity of childhood, then, is both about the constant presence of children in our world and how such a presence must remind us of the way childhood must be ubiquitous in our hearts.

PRINCIPLES FOR CHILDREN'S DISCIPLESHIP

Having identified five important ways in which the Scriptures touch on childhood, it is now time to think about how these themes might influence how we disciple our children. To do this, I have settled upon three principles to help guide our efforts. Each one is connected to a few of the themes already discussed and has practical implications, which I believe will be helpful.

The first principle of children's discipleship is *teaching for the life of faith*. Bringing together the themes of training and obedience, this principle invites us to consider the ways in which we are called to both impart wisdom and model actions that are part of the Christian life. Discipleship is not simply about what one knows, and it is not only about what one does. Rather, discipleship holds both together because the Christian life is focused ultimately not upon action or knowledge but on God's love.

As we respond to and live in God's love, we must grow in our knowledge of him and begin to act in the ways to which he is calling us. Herein lies the real work of children's discipleship: communicating these things to children in a way that will help them grow and remained fixed upon Christ. Such teaching and modeling might look different in various settings, but it must always be done with reference to the call of Christ to raise up disciples. No teaching style, program, curriculum, or approach to ministry can be considered too sacred to change; all must be modified as needed to best serve the goal of helping children to follow after him.

A book by Ivy Beckwith explains the ways in which teaching for the life of faith looks a little different in our contemporary world; it is entitled *Formational Children's Ministry*.[22] Beckwith lays out the importance of helping our young people inhabit the story of God's Word, encouraging us to let them do so in less guided and linear ways than many existing curricula might permit. Having students encounter the Bible on its own terms is a big part of this, and the practices and rituals of faith, as well as our Christian relationships, can reap great benefits as we disciple our younger brothers and sisters in faith. Beckwith's is only one approach to teaching for the life of faith, but she offers a wealth of innovations and the ability to move beyond the "same old."

A second principle is *developing an age-appropriate and progressing method*. Based mostly upon the transience of childhood, this principle reminds us that there is no "one-size-fits-all" method for children's ministry. Because of this, the task of the children's pastor is the most difficult in the entire church. While other ministers are dealing with the host of issues unique to those under their care, only the children's pastor is required to disciple a group whose members are in such vastly different developmental stages. The four-year-old and the ten-year-old could not be more dissimilar, and yet both are lumped together under the same ministry umbrella. Not only this, but even two children in the same age or grade may be at rather different points in their growth such that it can be difficult to adequately communicate in a way that reaches them both equally well.

Those who are called to disciple children must therefore pay keen attention to the design of the ministry and the ways in which teaching, worship, structure, and leadership take shape. Children's pastors must be aware of not only the differences among their students, but the methods that will best serve the needs of the various sub-groups represented. Additionally important is the appropriate selection of leaders best suited for different ages.

Though dated, the classic book *Stages of Faith* by James Fowler[23] can help provide children's pastors with some great insights into the development of faith processing within young people and provide insights into how best to minister to them. As children grow, their brain development and experience with others changes how they understand a host of things, including God. It is of great help to know this, not just in general, but also in some specific ways. I use the book regularly in a course I teach about discipleship and feel that it has real use for any minister, but especially those who are called to serve those under eighteen.

The third and final principle I will discuss in this chapter is *maintaining an orientation of thankfulness*. My thoughts here derive from the themes of blessing and ubiquity. Children are everywhere, and despite how frustrating that reality can be in the midst of a chaotic Sunday morning program, their presence is truly life-giving. The blessing that the Scripture speaks of is real. Though all of those we pastor are not our own, in those moments when we are with them God has truly placed them in our care.

Children have energy, vitality, and life that sometimes astound us. Even in those moments when this astonishment can veer into frustration, being reminded of the ways in which such exuberance for life persists and what a privilege it is to work with such blessed little people should make us thankful. This thankfulness means that we should never take for granted what we are doing and avoid giving into despair even when the road gets tough.

When we minister, we must also be deeply thankful to God for allowing us to be with those who provide such a great model of faith. As we are reminded of the ubiquity of childhood in our world, so too we are allowed many examples of how such faith and trust can arise in our hearts; this is the call to make childhood more ubiquitous in us, if you will. As we address the children in the midst of a Sunday morning program or special event, we can hear echoes of how John addresses his readers or of how God looks at us. As we see them respond to the Scripture with questions both simple and profound, we should praise God for what the model of true childlike faith looks like. Not everyone gets the opportunity to see childhood up close and personal, after all.

I have no book to recommend on this topic except for the living one: life with children. As parents and children's workers, we are engaging chapter after chapter as we teach, pray with, love, and serve kids. They are always there, and they have much to teach us about those things that should never fade from our own lives. The Irish rock star Bono once implored his listeners to please stay children somewhere in their hearts.[24] I can think of no better place to learn this principle than by working with the young. May we be thankful for the opportunity God has given us to do so. Though we grow older, new groups of children we serve will always be young, ever calling us to remember the gifts of youth.

CONCLUSION

When the Bible addresses the themes of obedience and training, we can apply its words directly to discipling children. However, themes such as ubiquity, transience, and blessing are more subtle. Still, taken together, all of these themes argue for the importance of discipling children.

As these themes begin to take the shape of principles, we are reminded that the way in which we approach childhood affects how we interact with them. In discipleship, it makes a difference if we approach our kids with thankfulness. God loves them. They are important. They have contributions to make. Woe unto us if we forget this. Part of our job in discipling them is to teach them to whom they belong and the implications for belief and action this has in their lives. May we be faithful and helpful guides to them along this journey.

We must be reminded that our children are in a state of flux. As ever changing and developing people, we must look to them and use our knowledge and experience to help them best understand, process, and work out their salvation in ways that are helpful to them at their level of faith.

Since the task of discipling children is not exhaustively detailed in the pages of the Bible, we need to probe more deeply into scriptural themes and principles in order to succeed. Scripture contains no extended discussion of how we are to run our programs and no "Book of Children's Ministry" among the letters of Paul. But thankfully we can glean important ideas from those places in Scripture where the idea of childhood is discussed, and they will help us as we move forward. May God bless us in this effort as we assist the upcoming generation in their journey of faith.

REFLECTION QUESTIONS

1. What is a core Bible passage you reflect on when you think about children's ministry? Why does it have such value for you?

2. What are the most difficult things to teach children? What are the easiest? What behaviors are the easiest for children to understand and learn? What are the most difficult?

3. If children's ministry is not about behavior modification, why do you think we should still be concerned about training and obedience?

4. How are you addressing developmental concerns in your ministry? What changes might you have to make to be more effective in addressing the various needs represented?

5. What have the children in your ministry taught you about faith and the life of discipleship?

6.

1.2 - KIDS BECOMING CHRISTIAN
Kate Thaete

KIDS NEED JESUS

I came to Christ as a teenager, and boy, did it seem to take forever to work out the basic obedience problems. But when I looked at my friends and leaders who loved Jesus, I saw such a difference compared to my own life. I knew I needed Jesus too.

The message of the gospel really boils down to one big concept: people need Jesus. Those who serve in ministry probably believe this already. It's easy for us to look at the structures, programs, systems, and ideas that make up our ministry world and see how they are tailored to *adults* who need Jesus.

We have adult worship services on the weekends. And kids go to programs that often get dubbed "childcare" (which makes me cringe).

During the week, we have adult small groups, community groups, home groups—whatever new name each church has come up with. And kids are shuffled off to play in the playroom, while the adults do the *real* work of growing spiritually.

Parents give their time to ministry teams at church, so they serve at the 9:00 AM service and attend the 11:00 AM service. That means their kids stay for two services, enduring the same lineup of object lessons and praise songs, bribed by leaders to not ruin the magic trick that they've already seen demonstrated at the earlier service. (Pastor's kids and deacon's kids are the most common offenders or, perhaps, victims.)

Why do ministry leaders go to such trouble to plan for adults? Because adults need Jesus. But kids need Jesus too. And if we really believe that, we should be moved to create a culture in our churches where our child-oriented ministries are known for providing meaningful encounters with Jesus instead of just childcare. We should find ways for families to create community *together,* where we're all doing the work of growing spiritually *together*—even the kids. What if our weekend kids' gatherings were tailored so that kids experiencing more than one gathering learned the same principle in a different way or were even involved in serving in a meaningful capacity themselves. Is it more work? Certainly. Is it worth it? Definitely. Why? Because kids need Jesus too.

CAN KIDS BE SAVED?

"They're just kids. They can't possibly understand salvation." I've heard this response, or some variation of it, more times than I can count. My instinct wants to reply "And you do?" But my filter engages in a timely fashion (years of practice), and instead I say, "Well, I doubt any of us *truly* understand salvation. But if Jesus encouraged us to have faith like a child, why can't kids be saved?"

I can picture the bright, sunny day. Jesus was surrounded by waves of people. The disciples just wanted his attention, but the people kept coming. And the nerve of these women who brought their children! Didn't they know who this was? The Great Teacher would never have time for children!

But Jesus scolded them, pointing out once again that they just didn't get it. God's Kingdom seems backwards compared to the ways of our world, but really, we are the ones who have it backwards. "Let the little children come to me. Don't hinder them. The Kingdom of God belongs to such as these. If you will not receive the kingdom of God like a child does, you will not enter it."[25] The disciples said "Children are nothing! Take them away." But Jesus said "Children are so important. Learn from *them*."

I love the way *The Message* phrases it: "Don't push these children away. Don't ever get between them and me. These children are at the very center of life in the kingdom. Mark this: Unless you accept God's kingdom in the simplicity of a child, you'll never get in."[26]

If we claim that children cannot be saved, we do that very thing Jesus warned us about. We get between them and him, just as the disciples did.

And in case the Bible isn't enough evidence, research supports Jesus' position. George Barna's book, *Transforming Children into Spiritual Champions* shows us that if a person is going to make a decision for Christ, he or she is most likely to do that before age thirteen.[27] After this, the likelihood of a person accepting Christ drops drastically. Barna says:

The probability of someone embracing Jesus as his or her Savior was 32 percent for those between the ages of 5 and 12; 4 percent for those in the 13–18 range; and 6 percent for people 19 or older. In other words, if people do not embrace Jesus Christ as their Savior before they reach their teenage years, the chance of their doing so at all is slim.[28]

Why does it seem so easy for a child to accept Christ? Perhaps it's that *childlike faith*. But what exactly is childlike faith? Is it the naiveté that will accept the Tooth Fairy, Santa Claus and the Easter Bunny without question?

Perhaps. But it seems more likely that Jesus is talking about a child's innate ability to accept truth without fully understanding it. That's simplicity.

A child can accept that their parents love them more than anyone else in the world. They don't even require the emotional investment that takes place during the pregnancy. A child can accept that *God made the earth* without understanding the role of the Trinity at the time of creation. A child can accept that there will always be food on the table at dinnertime without understanding the meal planning, the grocery shopping, or the long hours worked at the job mom or dad don't enjoy. They don't understand them but they do accept them. That's simplicity. And so too, a child can hear that God loves them and made them, that Jesus died for their sins, and a child can accept that truth without understanding how or why spiritual rebirth occurs. That's simplicity; that's wonder.

WHAT DOES SALVATION LOOK LIKE IN THE LIFE OF A CHILD?

So if anyone, no matter the age, can be saved, what needs to be in place in the child's heart before salvation can take place? These "requirements" are no different for a child than for an adult. Consider the following:

- A child should understand that he/she does wrong things, which we call "sin."
- A child should believe that Jesus took the punishment for his/her sins when He died on the cross.
- "If you declare with your mouth, 'Jesus is Lord,' and believe in your heart that God raised him from the dead, you will be saved."[29]

Is this a complete theology? No. Spiritual growth and time will flesh it out into something more comprehensive. But if any child, at any age, can be saved, then this is truly a matter of basics.

We might also wonder what evidence of salvation in a child's life looks like. This becomes more complicated, because we have to consider the child's own developmental progress. A four-year-old who says he loves Jesus and believes that Jesus is his Savior will still lie. That's part of the learning process of being four. Likewise, a twelve-year-old who loves Jesus will still struggle with some degree of rebellion and identity-establishment that accompanies becoming a teenager. So let's not assume that a child who is saved at age four will immediately be transformed into a mature Christian, any more than we should assume this for an adult saved at age forty-four. Transformation is a process; such processes look differently depending on where each individual begins his or her own metamorphosis.

But there's one other element here we should not overlook: the work of the Holy Spirit. It would be foolish to think that salvation is something *we* accomplish, in our lives, or in the lives of the children we influence. Salvation is by God's grace alone. Jesus said, "No one can come to me unless the Father who sent me draws them."[30] It is the work of the Holy Spirit that opens our hearts, enlightens our minds, and reshapes our will.

How Do we Lead Children to Christ?

Perhaps the theology of childhood salvation isn't an obstacle for many people. Instead, they get stuck trying to imagine exactly what to say, and they're not alone. They're right to sense the importance, the weight, the honor of being the influencer who shows children their need for Jesus. But let's remember that this only happens when the Holy Spirit has already paved the way. How do we lead children to Christ?—

- **Pray first**, and don't underestimate this step! We're prideful if we think we can lead someone to salvation without asking God's help.
- **Ask questions.** Build a relationship. You will be able to communicate the gospel to them in a more personal way if you understand where they're coming from.

- **Share the gospel in simple terms.** Karl Bastian, of kidology.org, calls this "the Bad News vs. the Good News." Show them the bad news: that we're all sinful, then give them the good news: that Jesus died for us so that we don't have to. Don't expect kids (or anyone for that matter) to get excited about Jesus until they understand their own need for him.

- **Read them the Bible** in an age-appropriate translation (we love the New Living Translation!).

- **Ask more questions** to discern if they understand the gospel, or if there are more opportunities for conversation. Avoid "christianese"—those words we use that only adult Christians would understand. You'll lose a kid if you start talking about being washed in the blood of the Lamb.

- **Pray with them.** If they're ready to ask Jesus to be in charge of their life, show them how with a simple repeat-after-me prayer. This isn't a matter of magic words, just expressing belief. Help the child admit that he is a sinner, that he believes Jesus died and rose again for him, that he wants to be saved, and that he needs God's help.

- **Celebrate.** This is an incredible experience for you and the most important day for them. Tell them what they've just done: they've given their lives to Jesus, and they are now a part of God's family forever.

- **Encourage and follow up.** Give them a Bible. Talk to their parents. Help them learn to pray, grow by reading their Bible, and get to church.

CLOSING SUMMARY

It's true that most individuals will make a decision for Jesus before they become teenagers, so let's get on it. I hope this chapter has helped conquer the hurdles of *how* and *if* kids can accept Christ as their Savior. Let's start figuring out how we can be more effective at helping kids who need Jesus.

Perhaps the best method for that comes from Jesus Himself. "Christ Jesus who died—more than that, who was raised to life—is at the right hand of God and is also interceding for us."[31] That word "interceding" is sometimes translated "pleading." What a picture that is—that Jesus sits next to God and pleads for us, asking for us to be given to Him. If we really believe that kids need Jesus, maybe we should try that. Let's plead with God to move these kids to Jesus.

REFLECTION QUESTIONS

1.   How old were you when you were saved? What effect do you think your age and life experience had on your willingness to accept Christ?

2.   If you were saved as a teen or an adult, do you know someone who gave his or her life to Christ as a child? What do you recall of their story?

3.   What did you have to discover before you could really give your life to Jesus? What was missing from your earlier understanding that delayed your salvation to a later age?

4.   What practical examples can you identify to show that a child may be saved, but still behaving like a child?

5.   How can we tell the difference between the actions of an unsaved child and the behavioral norms of a child's developmental stage?

1.3 - THE BIG DEAL ABOUT KIDS AND WORSHIP
David M. Cameron

A BUSY DAY INTERRUPTED

While sitting in the van waiting for my wife to come out of a store one day, I began reviewing the tasks that still needed to be completed at work, the people to be contacted, and the emails that had to go out. Our DVD player was occupying my three year old while my newborn baby slept. At that moment my fiveF yearF old decided to sing at the top of her lungs, the way only a fiveF yearF old can sing: slightly off key but totally confident.

I attempted to block her out and focus on my mental toF do list but there was no winning that battle so I turned to tell her to keep it down. Thankfully, before I said anything the words of her song began to penetrate my thoughts. She was singing the chorus of the song, "Today Is the Day," belting out a message of rejoicing in the day, trusting in Jesus, and rejoicing all the time.[32]

Her song stopped me in my tracks. Here I was caught up in the stress of my day, ready to tell my daughter to keep it down because she was interrupting my thoughts, and she was singing a song filled with a message of trusting God. Her song took me out of my own concerns and immediately made me think of Jesus' Sermon on the Mount:

For this reason I say to you, do not be worried about your life, as to what you will eat or what you will drink; nor for your body, as to what you will put on...who of you by being worried can add a single hour to his life...But seek first His kingdom and His righteousness, and all these thing will be added to you. So do not worry about tomorrow; for tomorrow will care for itself. Each day has enough trouble of its own."[33]

Here was the most amazing message ever preached, about trusting God and laying your worries upon the Lord for He is more than capable to handle all of them. And it was all caught up in a song sung a little bit off-key by a five-year-old girl who was singing simply because that is what you do when you know a song.

PURPOSE OF CHILDREN'S MINISTRY

This got me thinking about the importance of worship in our children's ministries. Each week we are given a gift: Parents drop off their kids so they can head to service and we are left with an opportunity to plant God's truth into the hearts of those kids. Sure, meetings don't always go as planned and survival can trump significance. But we must remember that time with those children is precious. We should do our very best with the opportunities we have and sow the most important seeds into the lives of those kids.

As children's pastors we are to partner with parents in the raising up of their children. While we are not the highest authority in their lives, we should go out of our way to support the authority that the parents have been given by God in every way possible. Proverbs 22:6 reminds parents to, "Train up a child in the way he should go, even when he is old he will not depart from it." Having said that, we do have a spiritual authority to come alongside parents and be as proactive as we can with the time that we are given. It is during that time at church every week that we help to train children in righteousness, so that when they are older they will not depart from that training.

This begs the question: What should we be doing with that time every week? We should be preaching the word of God, having fun with the kids, building community, memorizing Scripture, praying, playing games, and worshipping. I believe that several responsibilities as pastors should rise to the top: preaching, praying, and worshipping. In this chapter we will talk about worship.

WHY TEACH KIDS TO WORSHIP?

What makes worship one of those essential elements of children's ministry? When we have a weekly time allotment of sixty to ninety minutes to sow into the lives of those children why should we go out of our way sing a few songs? Would we be better served by spending more time helping the kids memorize Scripture or telling Bible stories? Perhaps we should be making sure to spend as much time in prayer as possible.

There are two important reasons why worship should become a vital component of your ministry: The Bible commands it, and worship teaches theology.

THE BIBLE COMMANDS US TO WORSHIP

God demands praises from his people, as Christians we are called to worship him:

> O come, let us sing for joy to the Lord, Let us shout
> joyfully to the rock of our salvation. Let us come before His
> presence with thanksgiving, Let us shout joyfully to Him with

psalms. . . . Come let us worship and bow down, let us kneel before the Lord our Maker. (Psalm 95:1–2, 6, NASB)

Let the word of Christ richly dwell within you, with all wisdom teaching and admonishing one another with psalm and hymns and spiritual songs, singing with thankfulness in your hearts to God. (Colossians 3:16, NASB)

Shout joyfully to the Lord, all the earth. Serve the Lord with gladness; Come before Him with joyful singing. (Psalm 100:1–2, NASB)

And do not get drunk with wine, for that is dissipation, but be filled with the Spirit, speaking to one another in psalms and hymns and spiritual songs, singing and making melody with your heart to the Lord. (Ephesians 5:18–19, NASB)

Sing to the Lord, all the earth; proclaim good tidings of His salvation from day to day. . . . For great is the Lord and greatly to be praised. (1 Chronicles 16:23–24, NASB)

As soon as He was approaching, near the descent of the Mount of Olives, the whole crowd of the disciples began to praise God joyfully with a loud voice for all the miracles which they had seen, shouting: "Blessed is the King who comes in the name of the Lord; Peace in heaven and glory in the highest!" Some of the Pharisees in the crowd said to Him, "Teacher, rebuke your disciples." But Jesus answered, "I tell you, if these become silent, the stones will cry out. (Luke 19:37–40, NASB)

As followers of Jesus Christ we are commanded to sing praises to God. One of the major facets of living that Christian life is worshipping God through singing, raising our hands, dancing, playing instruments, and so on. In fact our entire lives are to be offered to God *as a living sacrifice* so that when we come to a time of worship it should simply be an overflow of the heart.[34]

Children's pastors understand that we are coming alongside parents to help them train their children in righteousness and to follow the Lord. Teaching kids to worship should be a critical piece of what we do in our children's ministry time. That is not to say that it needs to be done in one particular way or that it even needs to be done every single week; rather, it needs to be taught intentionally. The question to ask is this: "What is the best way for us to teach the kids in our ministry how to worship God?" The answer may vary from church to church but what should be the same is a deep seeded resolve to make teaching our kids how to worship a priority in children's ministry for the purpose of training them in righteousness.

How Do We Teach Kids To Worship?

The biblical mandate stating that we should teach kids to worship leads to a practical question: *how do we do it?* One of the biblical ideas that was planted in my heart as a child was the presence of the different modes of worship in which we can engage.

Throughout the Psalms we discover nine tangible actions we are able to act upon in order to worship the Lord, these nine ways can be broken down into three sets of three. They include voice, body, and hands.[35] Let me unpack them for you here:

Voice—Speaking, Singing, Shouting

Speaking: I will bless the Lord at all times: His praise shall continually be in my mouth. (Psalm 34:1, NASB) Praise the Lord, all nations; laud Him, all peoples. (Psalm 117:1, NASB)

Singing: I will give thanks to the Lord according to His righteousness and will sing praise to the name of the Lord Most High. (Psalm 7:17, NASB). "Therefore I will give thanks to you among the nations, O Lord, and I will sing praises to your name (Psalm 18:49)." Sing praises to God, sing praises; Sing praises to our King, sing praises (Psalm 47:6)."

Shouting: And now my head will be lifted up above my enemies around me, and I will offer in His tent sacrifices with shouts of joy; I will sing, yes, I will sing praises to the Lord. (Psalm 27:6). Sing to Him a new song; play skillfully with a shout of joy. (Psalm 33:3, NASB). Shout joyfully to God, all the earth. (Psalm 66:1, NASB)

Body—Bowing, Standing, Dancing

Bowing: All the earth will worship You,[36] and they will sing praises to You; they will sing praises to Your name. (Psalm 66:4, NASB). Come, let us worship and bow down, Let us kneel before the Lord our Maker. (Psalm 95:6, NASB). I will bow down toward Your holy temple and give thanks to Your name for Your loving kindness and Your truth. (Psalm 138:2, NASB).

Standing: You who fear the Lord, praise Him; All you descendants of Jacob, glorify Him, and stand in awe of Him, all you descendants of Israel. (Psalm 22:23, NASB).[37]

Dancing: You have turned my mourning into dancing. (Psalm 30:11, NASB). Let them praise His name with dancing; Let them sing praises to Him with timbrel and lyre. (Psalm 149:3, NASB). Praise Him with timbrel and dancing; Praise Him with stringed instruments and pipe. (Psalm 150:4, NASB)

Hands—Raising, Clapping, Playing Instruments

Raising: So I will bless You as long as I live; I will lift up my hands in Your name. (Psalm 63:4, NASB). Lift up your hands to the sanctuary and bless the Lord. (Psalm 134:2, NASB)

Clapping: O clap your hands, all peoples; Shout to God with a voice of joy. (Psalm 47:1, NASB).

Playing Instruments: Give thanks to the Lord with the lyre; Sing praises to Him with a harp of ten strings. (Psalm 33:2–3, NASB). Praise Him with the trumpet sound; Praise Him with the harp and lyre. Praise Him with timbrel and dancing; Praise Him with stringed instruments and pipe. Praise Him with loud cymbals; Praise Him with resounding cymbals. Let everything that has breath praise the Lord. Praise the Lord! (Psalm 150:3–5, NASB)

Intentionally teaching these nine expressions of worship is great for kids because it offers tangible actions for them to focus on during times of worship. Not every expression of worship will be appropriate for each service and some may only be appropriate once in a while but they remain a biblical foundation that gives leaders the ability to teach and lead kids in the way they should worship.

Worship Teaches Theology

The other major reason why we should make worship a core part of our children's ministries is the fact that worship teaches theology. My daughter will very likely be worried at some point in her life, but because the song, "Today is the Day" is planted in her heart she knows that she doesn't need to worry about tomorrow; she can trust in what God says. She has that seed planted and growing deep down so that when worry pops up the Holy Spirit can remind her through song that when God is in charge of our life we do not have to worry.

Songs have a way of sticking in our minds for years; ask any adult who grew up in the church to sing "Jesus Loves Me." They may take a second to think, but inevitably they will know every single word and be able to sing the tune. As children's pastors we should take advantage of this by carefully choosing songs that are full of good theology and teaching them to the kids who come into our children's ministries.

Away In A Manger

When I was in Bible college a friend observed how Jesus was a normal human being and would have fussed and cried like any other baby. I confidently informed him that we know scripturally Jesus did not cry. My friend was taken aback and said he was pretty sure that was not in the Bible. I took out my concordance to find the verse I had read while I was a child and end the argument. Much to my chagrin that verse was not there and I had to admit that I was wrong.

For weeks I tried to figure out why I had believed the Bible taught that Jesus did not cry like other babies. It all clicked when I heard the old Christmas song, "Away in a Manger":

Away in a manger, no crib for a bed,

The little Lord Jesus lay down His sweet head,

The stars in the bright sky looked down where He lay,

The little boy Jesus asleep on the hay.

The cattle are lowing, the baby awakes

But little Lord Jesus no crying He makes.

I remembered hearing this song as a kid and coming to the conclusion that Jesus did not cry like other babies because, "little Lord Jesus no crying He makes." That line in an old Christmas song had embedded in me a theological belief about Jesus that I did not correct until years later.

Songs have that power, they get stuck in our head as catchy melodies, smuggling ideas and concepts into our mind. We find ourselves singing or humming without thinking about it and can quote the lyrics of a tune more easily than any other text. It is incumbent upon us as leaders then to make sure we choose songs with good theology.

CONCLUSION

As children's pastors we are called to partner with parents to help train their children in righteousness. Teaching kids to worship is one of the ways we accomplish this goal. Our mandate is to proactively teach kids how to worship God in a biblical way and choose songs that solidify good theological concepts in their hearts and minds.

REFLECTION QUESTIONS

1. List some of the songs you sing in your ministry. What are they teaching kids about Jesus?

2. How will you lead kids in worship with their voice, body, and hands?

3. How can you integrate a worship experience with an overall strategy for creating Jesus-followers in your ministry?

PART TWO: LEADERSHIP

Leadership is an essential part of pastoral ministries. As children's pastors, we often deal with the largest volunteer base in the church, and yet we are required to provide for the most dependent demographic in the entire church! Kids are counting on you to lead and you were called to lead, so start leading!

Dan Metteer starts us off with a discussion on "Discovering Vision, Mission, and Strategy." These words get thrown around a lot but what do they actually mean? Dan makes sense of it all and includes some great exercises at the end for you and your team. Dorene Heeter examines "Leadership Over Management" and presents a compelling case for our role as empowerers and not just doers. Chantel Rohr hits a home run when she writes about "Working With Volunteers." This discussion is practical, thoughtful, and will challenge you to do more when leading your teams.

2.1 - DISCOVER VISION, MISSION, AND STRATEGY
Dan Metteer

MISSION (UN)FOCUSED

I used to get frustrated when I heard people talk about their "mission and vision" for ministry. I would meet individuals who talked a lot about having a mission and vision but when it came down to specifics, it was hard for me to figure out what exactly they meant. When someone would ask what *my* vision for ministry was, I would panic. It felt like the person was putting me into a sudden job interview, or like I going to date their daughter and they wanted to hear what I had planned for my life. I did my best to fake it, but it was usually a rambling and confused answer.

I was pretty sure that I didn't have a vision—or if I did, I didn't know what it was. It made me feel like a failure. Good leaders had mission statements. Good leaders could express a clear and compelling vision. I had neither of these and came to the logical conclusion that I was not a good leader.

So if I had read a book on children's ministry that had a chapter on vision and mission, I might have been tempted to skip it—or at least skim through it—just to avoid feeling more discouraged than I already was. But I suggest that you resist that temptation! If any of what I have said echoes what you have thought about being a leader with a mission and a vision, I think I can help.

You are a person of purpose. And that means you are a person with a mission and a vision. The fact that you are reading this book probably means that you, at some point in your life, were radically changed by the God of the Universe. The day you said, "Yes" to Jesus was the day you left your old life behind and received a new life—a life of adventure, a life of passion, and a life of purpose (2 Corinthians 5:17–20). If you take your salvation seriously, then you are a person of purpose, a person whose life is built on mission.

And you have also chosen to minister to children. You are giving a big chunk of your life to do some hard work for low pay and little glory. So why do you do it? You do it because somewhere deep inside you there is a vision of what could be—what *should* be—and you want to take part in it.

Andy Stanley says that vision, "begins with the inability to accept things the way they are."[38] That is you. That's why you do this, right? Whether it was a God-given call, a moral imperative, or a feeling you couldn't shake, you decided to serve because the thought of a world in which you weren't serving just wouldn't do. And you have a vision of what could be, whether you can express it in words or not. You are serving, or leading, or giving to make that vision a reality. It is inside you—now all you have to do is get it out for the rest of us.

MAKING SENSE OF SCHINDLER'S LIST

A few years ago, I made a goal to watch every Academy Award winner for best picture. It was a great opportunity to catch some great films that I had missed. In the process, I checked out *Schindler's List* from the library—a movie I had heard great things about, but had never seen. I popped in the DVD and prepared myself for a great film. But to my surprise, this epic best picture began with—a list. It was Schindler reading a list of names... for a long time. "I guess this is why they call it *Schindler's List,*" I surmised. Still, it seemed like a strange way to start a film. Then I was surprised again when the movie ended in just over an hour, and during that whole hour I had absolutely *no idea* what was going on. In my bewilderment, I pulled out the DVD. It was then that I realized that this was a two-sided DVD. Part One was on one side, and on the other side (the side I had started with) was Part Two. Needless to say, "Schindler's List" made a lot more sense when I started it from the beginning.

This is how it is when you talk about vision. When you begin behind everyone else, the vision may not make much sense. You will nod your head and try to understand what everyone is saying, because (like me watching *Schindler's List*) you don't realize that you missed anything. All you know is you don't get it.

But when you are there from the beginning, everything is different.

THE MAGIC MOMENT

Do you remember that moment? Do you remember sitting down with a group of people and dreaming about what could be? It might have been a church plant, or your fresh entry into ministry, or just a huge goal that you decided you could achieve. You could see it so clearly. You got goose bumps. The hair stood up on your neck. Your heart beat faster, because you could hardly wait to get started. Anything was possible. No challenge mattered, because you knew what had to be done. Do you remember that moment? Maybe it wasn't with a group of people. Maybe, for you, it was listening to a speaker share his heart, or just you alone in your bedroom with your Bible. But we have all had that moment. That's the beginning. That's when everything makes sense.

When we talk about communicating a clear and compelling vision, this is what we are talking about—maintaining the way you felt, and spoke, and acted at the beginning when you knew exactly what needed to be done. The person who can bottle up the feeling of that moment and pour it out for others in a way that lets them feel the same excitement is the person who can communicate vision.

The problem with the excitement of the beginning, though, is that it doesn't last. Life happens. Obstacles may spring up in your path. Disappoint may come, and the temptation is to let the passion you once had fall to the ground as you keep moving forward, step by tedious step. Then when a string of people who weren't there at the beginning of the journey (when you used to be so excited) start asking, "What's your vision?" you've got nothing to give.

WHAT IS WHAT AGAIN?

One of the things that add unnecessary frustration to our thought process is misunderstanding the words that are being used, so let's come to terms.

Mission. The mission is simply what you are trying to do. It's the main objective. If you are bowling, your mission is to knock down all of the pins. If you are playing tag, your mission is to tag someone, and then run like mad so you don't get tagged back. Mission doesn't speak to how, it doesn't speak to why, it just answers the question, "What should I be doing?"

As Christians, we all have the same mission. It's God's mission. We might not all state it in the same way, but our mission is the mission Jesus gave us—to love God, love others, and make disciples (Matthew 22:36–40; 28:16–20). It sounds simple, but being sure of your mission makes all of the difference. The mission is what lights the spark for the vision.

Vision. Vision is the clear and inspiring way that you are going to accomplish the mission. The mission is generally the same for all Christians, while the vision, although it is given by the same God, will be yours alone. Vision doesn't exactly answer the question, "What?" or even the question, "How?" Vision speaks more to the questions, "Where?" and, "Why?" "Where are we going, what is it going to look like when we get there, and why is it important that we do it right now?" These are the questions that vision answers.

Let's pause here for a minute. Those questions might seem trite, but think about the leader who ignores those questions:

- "Where are we going?" *I'm not exactly sure.*
- "What is it going to look like when we get there?" *How am I supposed to know?*
- "Why is it important that we do it now?" *I guess it is not, really, but we have to do something, right?*

Do you want to follow a leader like that? Neither do I.

Strategy. Strategy answers the "How" question in very specific terms. On the surface, this seems like the hardest part, but if everything else is done well, it should actually be the easiest. If the leader is communicating vision clearly, then strategy can be handed off, divvied up to teams of other leaders who can use their own gifts and abilities to see it through. If the strategy element is missing or not working well, one of three things is going wrong:

1. The leader has not cast a clear vision. This can actually be a bit of a litmus test for your vision. If the strategy that your team employs to accomplish your vision is routinely out of line with how you think things should be done, it probably means that your vision was not clearly understood in the first place. Remember, people are very likely to tell you that they understand you even if they don't. In fact, the moment someone asks you to clarify something is the moment they are just beginning to understand. The leader's job is to constantly recast and reinforce vision. If this is done well, strategy will come into line.

2. Insufficient time has been taken by the team to answer the question, "How?" In the busyness of life and ministry, important things often get overlooked. The visionary leader has to encourage his or her team to ask themselves the question, "How are we going to get this done?" The leader doesn't have to give the answer, but if he or she does not lead the team to think about strategy, it will often get missed.

3. The leader has not been willing to hand off strategic leadership. Remember the magic moment? The moment when no obstacle was too great to keep you from accomplishing your vision? In that moment you think you can do it all yourself. News flash: you can't. The sooner you realize that you need the time and skills of others to accomplish your vision, the sooner you will be on the road to making it a reality.

When leaders keep every important decision for themselves, they limit the people they work with from joining in whole-heartedly to the vision, employing their own God-given strengths and gifts to make it happen (1 Corinthians 3:6; 12:1–31).

Your *most* important job as a leader is to keep the picture of what could be in front of your people. When others work with you toward that same vision you win—and the Kingdom of God wins. Don't keep it to yourself.

THE POWER OF THE RIGHT WORDS

In Bill Hybels' book, *Leadership Axioms,* he illustrates the power of using the right words. "Sometimes whole visions live or die on the basis of the words the leader chooses for articulating that vision."[39] Hybels says that he will spend long periods of time walking around his church campus just to come up with one word to communicate what he wants to say in a way that thoroughly speaks the vision that he feels inside.

One of the values that his church has is to be compassionate. That is a good value. That should stir people to excitement. But unfortunately, it doesn't. "Be compassionate" sounds bland and predictable. So instead, Hybels and his team say they have a vision to, "unleash unprecedented amounts of compassion into our broken world."[40] Wow, that certainly conveys a different tone.

Another of Willow Creek's values is to have a strong evangelistic focus. But again, there is no passion in those words. So instead, they say they want to, "raise the level of risk in our attempt to point people to faith in Christ."[41]

Do you hear it? Do you hear how those words inspire action? "Be evangelistic" feels like a rule we are forced to follow. But "raise the level of risk" is a call to action. It is a battle cry. It is something that I want to be a part of.

Choosing the right words can paint the picture of what you felt at the beginning of your vision story without having to tell the whole story. This is a biblical principle: "And the Lord answered me: 'Write the vision; make it plain on tablets, so he may run who reads it'" (Habakkuk 2:2, ESV). When you can put the vision into the words that can truly express what you feel, the vision takes on legs of its own. It is worth it to put in the time to put your vision into precise and passion-filled statements. They make all the difference.

WHAT IF I'VE LOST IT?

At some point you felt a passion for what you are doing. But maybe you never articulated exactly what you felt. Or maybe you have faced so many disappointments and defeats that there is nothing left of the vision you once had. How do you get it back? It sounds like a difficult question, but there are some very simple things you can do to help bring that inspiration back:

1. Write in a journal. Writing down your thoughts on a regular basis can do two things. First, it can help you process some of the things that you are feeling but have not been able to put into words. And second, writing

down what inspires you, what frustrates you, what gives you hope, and what makes you angry over a period of time can actually paint a picture of the vision that God is birthing in you that you may not be able to see by just looking at the context of one day.

2. Talk it through with someone. Living inside your own head can be a lonely place. Finding someone to talk to—someone you can trust, not someone who you are going to have to try to impress—can help immensely in forming your vision. Having a friend who can coach you through questions that will challenge you to think and inspire you to dream is a priceless gift.

3. Visit someone else's ministry environment. Okay, I am not suggesting that you go to another church and copy their vision statement. But there is something exhilarating about seeing another ministry in action. It is hard to explain why this makes such a difference, but it does. Try it. Call up another church and ask them if you can tour their facility or sit in for a service. Sometimes you walk away ready to reach for new heights; other times you feel affirmed that your own strategies are on the right track. They will be flattered that you want to come, and you will be inspired.

4. Pray. I saved this one for last because I know it is tempting to brush it off. The importance of prayer cannot be overstated when it comes to forming your vision. Proverbs 3:5–6 says, "Trust in the Lord with all your heart, and do not lean on your own understanding. In all your ways acknowledge him, and he will make straight your paths" (ESV).

Notice that this passage does not only instruct us to trust in the Lord, but it also commands us *not* to lean on our understanding. All good direction comes from God, not from us.

YOUR VOTE OF CONFIDENCE

If you feel inadequate to be a leader who leads with vision, let me say this—first of all: good! You *are* inadequate. It's not you, it's God (1 Corinthians 1:26–31). But second, don't forget that God has positioned you where you are for a reason. 1 Corinthians 12:18 says, "But as it is, God arranged the members in the body, each one of them, as he chose" (ESV).

God has chosen your gifts, your personality, and your story to lead where you are. So go to it! You are a person of purpose, a person of passion, and leader with vision.

REFLECTION QUESTIONS

1. Can you clearly describe the mission, vision, and strategy of your ministry?

2. Can members on your team do the same? How do you determine if they actually *get it?*

3. Who can analyze your mission, vision, and strategy and offer you critical feedback? When are you going to set up a meeting with this person?

2.2 - LEADERSHIP OVER MANAGEMENT
Dorene Heeter

DEFINING YOUR ROLE

What is the exact role of the children's pastor, director or leader at a church? It has to do with the one thing that children's pastors need most— volunteers. It is a synonymous thought, like ice cream and cake, right? Or maybe your thoughts travel to hard work and sweat instead. However you look at it, recruiting and empowering volunteer teams is a big part of what we do.

Perhaps you've asked yourself some of the following questions: Just how do we mobilize volunteers? How can I effectively equip God's people to do his work? What does it look like to have various teams working with "all oars in the water"? These next few pages will begin to help you answer those questions.

Maybe you're experienced in recruiting but are challenged with leading the team and taking them to the next level. Leaders can experience a struggle and a natural pull toward over-management, which adversely affects teams and can cause ministries to lose momentum. We must intentionally balance both leadership and management in ministry, as both are needed.

Take a close look at Ephesians 4:11–13:

Now these are the gifts Christ gave to the church: the apostles, the prophets, the evangelists, and the pastors and teachers. Their responsibility is to equip God's people to do his work and build up the church, the body of Christ. This will continue until we all come to such unity in our faith and knowledge of God's Son that we will be mature in the Lord, measuring up to the full and complete standard of Christ. (NLT)

Christ is the one who has given his church the gifts of leadership so that we can function and be a healthy body of believers that will impact the world! That places a great responsibility on pastors and teachers. In verse 11, we can see that they are paired together, suggesting that the two roles complement each other. The pastors and teachers (shepherds) are entrusted with the nurture, protection and supervision of the church body (the flock), both young and old. Their appointment to leadership and call to ministry is for the good of the entire body of Christ. Each has a special role given by God with a clear imperative to equip and release others to do ministry.

In verse 12 we see that the aim of our ministry is "to prepare" or "put right."[42] In other words, our equipping helps people become aligned to God's purposes and mission. We are to lead them in such a way that they grow in their walk with God and become complete in Christ. When we see our role as a shepherd, we hone our skills to best lead the people that are in our church. We guide them in their God-journey and help them find fulfillment in serving, which in turn unifies the body toward a common purpose of obedience to the Great Commission. Verse 13 reveals the clearest reason for our ministry. We are to help people to grow in their understanding and experience of God and become mature Christians. Pastors and teachers must be leaders and managers in order to effectively accomplish this.

Wow! Just trying to comprehend all that those three verses hold is both exciting and challenging to a leader and even more so to a children's pastor. We minister to kids and adults—parents and volunteer teams (and perhaps paid staff members). We are asked to pastor three groups of people at all different age levels and different places in their Christian walk. Once you factor in other pastoral responsibilities to the larger church leadership team, that the challenge can begin to feel daunting!

Here is where we need to seek God's help daily and ask for his wisdom, just like King Solomon, to lead "this great people of His." Additionally, we need to establish a system of recruitment and training for our team that empowers and releases them to your church's "dream team," so that you as the leader are not doing ministry alone, nor limiting the kind of impact children's ministries can have in your church and community. You must lead people by casting the vision, then recruit and train a team to accomplish the vision, all the while providing the processes and tools to get the job done.

INVITE: OUT OF RELATIONSHIP AND GIFTING

When we recruit, let's change our vocabulary and adopt the concept of *invitation:* we are inviting others to join us in accomplishing the church's mission. Our invitations must be wrapped in our desire to equip and train others as highly effective volunteers. In other words, "join our kids' team and we will provide training, resources, coaching, support, and place you on a team; for no one does ministry alone!"

We also need to be certain that we are recruiting members who can use the gifts and talents that God has given them. Find a simple spiritual gifting survey to aid you and them. They will find more joy, be more faithful, and be awesomely creative when serving in ways that truly are a good fit for them. Ultimately they will find the greatest fulfillment and maturity as Christ-followers when serving, and we will be following Ephesians 4, which is the best prescription for success as pastors and teachers.

Couple your invitations to serve with the knowledge that you must invest in individuals. Out of relationship and friendship come the best recruitment opportunities. Be relational and get to know people in order to see abilities or qualities in them. Also, be particularly picky about the people you bring into your team. Seek out quality, passion, receptiveness, and the best overall fit. I am not saying that every person will come fully trained, but that people who make up your team should reflect both interest and talent to work with children and their parents. In order to do this you must interview prospects, match their gifting and invite them personally (forget spamming the church program).

Allow me to share the story of the Victors. They were a young couple who had recently moved into the area and had been attending our church for about three months. I would regularly greet them as they checked in their children and ask if I could have lunch or coffee with them. Over the course of a meal, I asked them to share their story and how they came to Christ. I heard and saw leadership qualities, creativity and a love for kids (they had three of their own). With joy in their eyes they asked if there was anything they could do to get more connected to people (note: not ministry or volunteering) and that they wanted something to do. I inquired about their passions, interests, and skills and was confident that they would be an awesome fit on the team. I invited them to join the team and begin making a difference in the lives of kids and parents. Two weeks after filling out the necessary application they started serving with our kids. I continued to coach and challenge them, meeting regularly with my team members and connecting with them. The following year the husband asked me if he could do an apprenticeship with me, as he was feeling called into ministry. This developed because of my relationship with the family. I loved them, connected them to other people (who happen to all serve in children's ministries), and invested in them as individuals and leaders. They are now thriving as children's pastors at another local church.

I love a happy ending, don't you? We must be prepared to invest a lot of time and resources into others so that they discover how God made them and how he wants them to serve. It requires intentionality in how we invite and connect God's people to serving.

INVOLVE: NEXT UP? GEN Z

What about those growing up in your church and ministry today, those pre-teens and incoming sixth- or seventh-graders? They represent a gold mine of volunteer potential. Somewhere during fourth or fifth grade, children desire to assume leadership roles. They say something like this: "I need to put my hands to what my heart already knows—I want to serve God and make a difference!" We might prefer the steady adults or older youth, but the reality is that *the next generation wants to connect and serve.* We need to invite and invest in them when they are asking, willing, and available. Andy Stanley makes the case well for having children start serving at a young age:

We are committed to involving as many people as possible, as young as possible, as soon as possible. Sometimes too young and too soon! But we intentionally err on the side of too fast rather than too slow. We don't wait until people feel "prepared" or "fully equipped." Seriously, when is anyone ever completely prepared for ministry?

Ministry makes people's faith bigger. If you want to increase someone's confidence in God, put him in a ministry position before he feels fully equipped."[43]

You may also find that those children who started in kindergarten in your kids' church are some of the quickest to understand your vision and heart for ministry, and they know what excellence looks like because they have been watching as you and your team minister to them every week. You have modeled ministry and they want to emulate your leadership! One of the best models follows this simple formula:

1. Watch me do it,
2. Help me do it,
3. I watch you do it,
4. You do it.

Invite them young and raise them up to be the next leaders. They will have opportunities to discovering their gifts in KidMin, music ministry, or in youth ministries. And who can forget serving as greeters, ushers, and media team for the main service? Paul said, "Follow me as I follow Christ!" Lead by example and invite the next generation to follow Jesus missionally and passionately.

INVEST: TIME AND RESOURCES

Do you ever feel overwhelmed by the enormity of all that you need to accomplish between Sundays? How do you find the time to invest in others? You plan the time and capture life-moments. You have to put it in your calendar and on your phone alarms. Scheduling time for people is one of the most important things you can do.

My husband is a quality manager for a nonprofit aerospace company and he recently told me that he put a weekly meeting on the team's calendar that is for connecting, communicating, and building relationships with one another. You read that right; the meeting is not for planning or doing, but for team-building; it is a specific time for people to connect and share their stories. He also said that the more time he spends in meetings with his team, the less he has to get done on his list. Mind you, I know he does a ton of work on his own, but how revealing his statement is. Time spent with others shows them you care about them as individuals, and that you want to help them be all God designed them to be. The result is trust and a sense of belonging that motivates and propels people forward.

Not making time for your team is #2 out of 10 in an article entitled, "10 of the Most Common Leadership and Management Errors, and What You Can Do to Avoid Them" by MindTools.com:

When you're a manager or leader, it's easy to get so wrapped up in your own workload that you don't make yourself available to your team.

Yes, you have projects that you need to deliver. But your people must come first—without you being available when they need you, your people won't know what to do, and they won't have the support and guidance that they need to meet their objectives.

Avoid this mistake by blocking out time in your schedule specifically for your people, and by learning how to listen actively to your team. Develop your emotional intelligence so that you can be more aware of your team and their needs, and have a regular time when "your door is always open," so that your people know when they can get your help.

Once you're in a leadership or management role, your team should always come first. This is, at heart, what good leadership is all about![44]

Your team needs you to *invest resources* into them and the ministry they are serving in. Once your new recruits are in place, some of the best questions to ask each time you meet with them are, "Do you have what you need? Is there something that would aid you in better accomplishing your ministry? How can I best help you to succeed?"

When a conference opportunity comes across your desk, ask yourself, "Which ones can I take along? Who would benefit most from the workshops or general sessions?" Personally invite them to attend and invest financially in them by paying for some part of the conference. I know that when they invest themselves and pay for the registration they will actually get more out of the event and they will not easily back out of going.

When a book catches your eye, buy one or more extras to give to team members. Investing in your team in this way will challenge and stretch them as leaders. People love gift cards and it is a simple way of investing in people by saying, "thank you, here's a cup of coffee." Invest in new resources. Ask your departments or teams to give you a list each quarter or year of items that need to be replaced or improved. You love your new phone, your team loves their new gadgets, and the kids will love the "new tech" that you buy and use on Sunday mornings, too.

Put each of the investment items mentioned in your budget. You must plan to invest or you will feel that you can't. You must have that budget conversation with your pastor and ask to increase your budget each year. Incrementally increasing the budget will allow you to purchase the tools and appreciation items you need. Being a leader means having vision for your ministry that is God-sized, believing for greater things and asking God to increase your faith in this area. He invests in us so that we can invest in others.

A final thought on investing in others: one of the best investments of a leader's time is to *inspect what you expect*. Andy Stanley says that, "Experience alone doesn't make you better at anything. Evaluated experience is what enables you to improve your performance."[45] Your volunteers need the opportunity to re-interview with you. About six to eight weeks into their new assignment, sit down with them and ask them how it is going and if they are finding their new position fulfilling or if they are struggling. What do they like and dislike? What is going well and not so well? Finding the answers to these questions will not only help you identify their challenges so that you can better equip them, but it also lets the volunteers know that you care about their spiritual growth. Remember, we want them to succeed and feel they are on the "dream team." If people are left in a position they don't feel fits them, they will quit and not readily volunteer for another position anytime soon. Our mission is to equip the church for works of service. Every person in the body of Christ has been given gifts and talents; let's help them discover the best fit for them.

VISION: DREAM BIG, STATE IT, REPEAT IT, HAVE COURAGE

Andy Stanley is a "visioneer" and, many would say, one of the greatest pastors of our time. He defines the term *vision* as "a mental picture of what could be, fueled by a passion of what should be."[46] Andy also clarifies the leader as one who...

...instills courage in the hearts of those who follow. This rarely happens through words alone. It generally requires action. Somebody has to go first. By going first, the leader furnishes confidence to those who follow. It is impossible to lead without a dream. When leaders are no longer willing to dream, it is only a short time before followers are unwilling to follow."[47]

As ministry leaders we often feel obliged need to leave the vision stuff to the senior pastor; at the least, we may feel that our ministry dream opportunities are limited because we serve in the shadow of others. Yes, our vision must be in alignment with that of our senior pastor and our church's mission and values. However, we must also have our own vision for our ministry, for our team, for our students and the families of our church, and for reaching those far from God in our community. Scripture clearly tells us that without vision the people "perish" (Proverbs 29:18). Those whose vision is fueled by passion for the mission will see God-sized dreams accomplished by faith! Without it, you cannot build confidence or lead a team.

Another truth is that *vision deflates over time and often more quickly than we realize.* A good leader continues to keep the vision in front of the team by myriad forms of communication. I value preparedness kits and items that you purchase before to have on hand and ready for disasters, both small and big. Once, I had just been dropped off at my car where I had parked for the day while attending a children's conference. I got in the car, turned on the ignition and the tire notification light came on immediately. Upon inspection, I saw that my front left tire was flat. I was far from home and even help. I looked in the back of my car for the spare tire and there it was—a can of "Fix It Flat." (Thanks, husband of mine!) I filled up the tire, following the instructions with care, and I made it all the way home.

Like a car tire, our vision is at risk of going flat and incapacitating our ministry. The feelings that accompany the flat tire range from a sigh of frustration to full fear! The team may not notice the leak at first and perhaps you will not even hear the small *fizzzzy* sound coming from the tire, but the reality is the tire will go flat in time if it's not refilled or fixed. The same is true with vision-casting. It needs to be monitored and refilled regularly. You will need to state the vision clearly, simply, and repeatedly. If you do, people will follow, your team will grow, and the lives of children and their families will be impacted. Be the leader by allowing God to give you dreams that only faith in Him can accomplish and by repeating the vision to your team with clarity and passion—with solid courage. As Andy Stanley writes:

The leader is the one who has the courage to act on what he sees. A leader is someone who has the courage to say publicly what everybody else is whispering privately. It is not his insight that sets the leader apart from the crowd. It is his courage to act on what he sees, to speak up when everyone else is silent. The first person to step out in a new direction is viewed as the leader. And being the first to step out requires courage. In this way, courage establishes leadership. Many who lack the courage to forge ahead alone yearn for someone to take the first step, to go first, to show the way. It could be argued that the dark provides the optimal context for leadership. After all, if the pathway to the future were well lit, it would be crowded. Fear has kept many would-be leaders on the sidelines, while good opportunities paraded by. They didn't lack insight. They lacked courage. Leaders are not always the first to see the need for change, but they are the first to act. Leadership is about moving boldly into the future in spite of uncertainty and risk. You can't lead without taking risk. You won't take risk without courage. Courage is essential to leadership. [48]

The leadership in children's ministry determines not only present approaches (management and maintenance) but should also position the ministry for the future (leadership and vision). Here is a table that more clearly illustrates the roles and traits of managers and leaders:

LEADERSHIP VS. MANAGEMENT PERSONALITY TRAITS[49]

Leaders	Managers
Big Picture	Detail Oriented
Strategic	Tactical
"Are We in the Right Jungle?"	Cutting Trees Efficiently
Vision, Strategy, Execution	Goals, Projects, Tasks
Effectiveness	Efficiency
Forge Vision	Follow Vision
Right Brain / Lateral Thinking	Left Brain / Linear Thinking

John Gilman succinctly describes leaders and managers in a great article:

> There's a lot out there on church leadership and management. There's a difference. Managers have one eye on yesterday, leaders have one eye on tomorrow, and together they have two eyes on today. They balance energy and efficiency. In the dance of day to day decisions, leaders take initiative and guide the steps. A church with a strong management team and no leadership coasts on stale vision.

A church with no leaders fades into irrelevance. A church with a strong leadership team and no management expertise generates excitement and accelerates people into ministry. . . but if no one manages the change, the organization can burn out. Leaders move hard and fast, but they wear out because they aren't doing things efficiently.[50]

The manager's job is to plan, organize and coordinate. The leader's job is to inspire and motivate. In his 1989 book *On Becoming a Leader,* Warren Bennis composed a list of the differences:

- The manager administers; the leader innovates.
- The manager is a copy; the leader is an original.
- The manager maintains; the leader develops.
- The manager focuses on systems and structure; the leader focuses on people.
- The manager relies on control; the leader inspires trust.
- The manager has a short-range view; the leader has a long-range perspective.
- The manager asks how and when; the leader asks what and why.
- The manager has his or her eye always on the bottom line; the leader's eye is on the horizon.
- The manager imitates; the leader originates.
- The manager accepts the status quo; the leader challenges it.
- The manager is the classic good soldier; the leader is his or her own person.
- The manager does things right; the leader does the right thing.[51]

Peter Drucker once wrote, "The task is to lead people. And the goal is to make productive the specific strengths and knowledge of every individual." Children's ministry leaders need to understand the type of leader they are and find ways to keep the vision "full." They are also called to be managers, equipping people to do the ministry and keeping the details of children's ministries organized and flowing. We can be stronger in one area and enlist the help of others to balance our weaknesses, but we must examine how God has wired us and acknowledge that both leadership and management are needed in children's ministry.

The challenge for each of us is this: discovering what God is calling you to do right now, for this time and in this church and community, that will transform the lives of kids and families for Christ. Do it by managing and leading the people who are already or yet to be invited onto your team and fulfill all that God has for you on His "dream team" of ministers.

REFLECTION QUESTIONS

1. What are the major differences between *leadership* and *management?* Which one do you practice most often?

2. How well have you defined your role as a leader? Can you write down your own job description including the things you must and must not do?

3. How are you investing into your teams? What type of investment can you make into another person today?

2.3 - WORKING WITH VOLUNTEERS
Chantel Rohr

MY STORY

Before I started college there were two things I said I'd "never" do: marry a pastor or become a pastor. Well, I struck out on both! It all began when I met Brad Rohr at Northwest University. I never imagined that he would one day become the love of my life. We graduated in 2007w he became a pastor, and I earned my Washington State teaching certificate for elementary education. In May of 2008 we tied the knot and became Mr. and Mrs. Rohr, the first on my list of "nevers" crossed off! After being married for eight months we felt God moving our family, but didn't realize how much that move would change our lives. A year and a half later I became the interim children's pastor at the same church where my husband was on staff. It was supposed to be a short threeF month position. When three months was up and they still hadn't found a new children's pastor, the lead pastor asked me to stay on longer. Around that time I had decided to attend a children's ministry conference with the Northwest Ministry Network.

With the decision to continue in the interim position weighing heavily on my mind and feeling the burden of leading the team as an interim pastor, I arrived at the conference and told God, "I'm going to shut up and let you speak to me." It was at that moment that God said, *"Finally!"* That conference was the beginning of God changing my heart and calling me to be a children's pastor. Second on my "never" list had failed! I went home and put my name in for the children's pastor position. After almost a year as interim pastor, I became the official children's pastor. This opportunity has taught me a lot about trusting in God and how to rebuild a hurting ministry into a healthy growing ministry with a strong team of volunteers.

THE LEARNING CURVE

Chances are if you are reading this you've been or are currently a volunteer. If that is the case, you should be an expert at leading volunteers, right? You know how it feels when a leader encourages and supports you, and you remember how it feels when a leader devalues you or leads poorly. Building on those experiences and becoming the type of leader you would follow should make working with volunteers a piece of cake, right? Wrong! When I first came on as the interim pastor I remember thinking, "I've got this! I've been a volunteer in children's ministry for over ten years." Boy, was I wrong!

While I believe my experiences have been very helpful, I learned that it's important to remember not everyone is like me, because each person has his or her own needs. Working with volunteers is very enjoyable, but differences in personality and opinion can make leading them challenging and stressful as well. So what does it look like to get over this learning curve and create a strong and growing ministry?

In this chapter we are going to focus on three main ideas: how you serve the volunteers you have, where to find volunteers, and how to start building a team. Leading a team of volunteers in children's ministry is tough, regardless of how much experience you've had. Hopefully this chapter will bring inspiration, help you refocus, and provide tips and steps to strengthen you as a leader of volunteers!

How do you serve the volunteers you have?

The best way to answer this question is by asking your volunteers how you can serve them. As I have asked volunteers over the years, I have found that there are three main ways that often resurface no matter whom I ask. These three ways include clearly communicating vision and expectations; providing appropriate training, equipment, and materials; and making them feel valued as individuals. In this section, we are going to dissect these ideas to help you serve your volunteers better.

Clearly communicating expectations and vision to your team is vital for their success as a whole and as an individual. How are they supposed to act, dress, or communicate with you, their teammates, children, and parents? What policies are enforced for the safety of the children and volunteers? What is the protocol for children who are acting out, ill, having a seizure? What if there's a restraining order against a family member? How does "check-in" work? What do you do if a child needs help in the restroom? These are just a few of the questions that may come up, and your volunteers need to have the knowledge and confidence to know what to do.

How will you communicate these expectations to your team? One of the ways I communicated these guidelines was through writing a children's ministry manual and handing it out at the annual fall training or to new recruits when they came in for their screening process. Make sure that your physical copy is accompanied with a digital one as well. This allows your team to quickly access policies, and protocols. Not everyone will read the manual thoroughly so it is important to communicate through trainings as well. During these trainings I give a quick review on key topics such as appropriate touch, restroom policies, or any other policies I feel needed to be reviewed. I model protocols, present different scenarios, and have discussions on what to do in certain situations.

Volunteers also want to know the heart of the ministry and where it's going. Having a clear vision helps them identify with what they are supporting. They will follow a vision that they feel passionate about. Every time I recruit a new volunteer, I give the individual a copy of the vision and core values, and we talk about what they mean. As a team, we gather once a year for a fun vision night where we can celebrate the past year and dream together for the upcoming year. This is a great opportunity to build relationships and review the overall vision for children's ministry.

Providing your volunteers with the appropriate training, equipment, and materials allows them to feel confident in what they are trying to accomplish. Trainings can come in many forms. You can take volunteers to workshops or conferences, put on your own training sessions with individuals who have skills and experience to help train your team, or work with other churches and present a two-hour workshop on certain topics (working with kids with special needs, classroom management, object lessons, etc.).

It is also important for you to have flexibility to roam during services so you can give real-time coaching to your volunteers. What does that look like? Church has started, children are checked in, and the teacher has begun the lesson. I quietly enter a room and sit among the children. During this time I am observing my teammates, as well as setting an example for kids by participating in the lesson. After about fifteen or twenty minutes I sneak out unobtrusively and then I briefly connect with them after the service. This allows me to encourage them, provide feedback (positive as well as constructive criticism), give suggestions, and allow them to ask questions.

When you talk about equipment and materials, each church will have access to different supplies. One of the best tools for volunteers is a curriculum that is easy to use. I understand that some churches are unable to purchase curriculum; if that is the case you may see if an individual or a group would be willing to sponsor a quarter or even a year's worth of curriculum. You can also connect with other churches to see if they would donate or allow to you to trade or buy used curriculum for a low price. If none of these options work, you can always help your volunteers by giving them a big idea to focus on, a memory verse, and a Bible story. It is important to give them the curriculum or plans in advance so they have time to look it over and pray throughout the week before they teach. Be sure to provide the items needed for the activities listed in the curriculum or plans. These items sometimes come with curriculum or can be donated if it is not in your budget. If you are unable to get certain supplies, have an alternative and clearly communicate the change with your volunteers. There is nothing worse than spending time planning for a lesson and then not being able to do what you spent so much time preparing for because supplies were unavailable. Remember to tap resources online; several groups publish free materials or ideas that can be helpful to you and your team.

The most important thing you can do is place a high value on the individual volunteer. People care if you care and there are several simple ways to show your concern. One of the simplest ways to show them is to genuinely ask the individual how he or she is doing. This means stopping, even in your rush, looking the person in the eyes, and actually listening. One of my team members once said, "When a leader takes the time to ask how I'm doing and is more concerned about my well-being than filling a ministry spot, that inspires me to be spiritually healthy." Remember that your volunteers are real people. It is so easy to run over people and forget they have real feelings, desires, passions, problems, and hurts. Take the time to acknowledge them and meet them where they are: broken and in need of Jesus, just like you.

Another great question to always ask is "How can I help you?" Every volunteer is unique and his or her needs are different. This question will help you support each volunteer the way he or she needs. Food, small gifts, and thank-you or thinking-of-you cards are never a bad idea either! Many churches host annual volunteer appreciation nights. These are a great idea and have a compounded impact when each department pools resources to say "thank you." Know that these public displays of appreciation can become an important factor for those considering to join your team as well. Let people see you say thank you, and say it often.

WHERE DO VOLUNTEERS COME FROM?

When people think about who can be a children's ministry volunteer, many minds quickly jump to that sweet old lady who has been teaching or rocking the babies in the nursery for thirty years. Although every leader loves and needs those kinds of volunteers, it's important to think outside the box. You will need a variety of personalities and skills to fill the different roles in children's ministry. So where do you find volunteers? The obvious answer is inside your church doors, but it is never that simple. To find more volunteers, you'll need to get out of your ministry area. Stop by the youth group to see if there are any junior high or high school students who could get plugged in. Visit life groups or seniors' potlucks to see if they would be willing to donate to a project for children's ministry. Pick older elementary age children to be junior helpers in the preschool class; or ask military service men or women to provide security for children's ministry areas.

Have you ever been told, "I wish I could help, but I'm not good with kids"? I have been told that too many times to count. At first, I didn't know how to respond to that comment. Then I began to ask myself, "What are ways people can serve outside of the classroom setting?" I came to find there were a lot of ways to engage more people in what God was doing in children's ministry. I was able to put together teams for donations, curriculum prep, monthly classroom organizers, and a cooking team that would bless our team by preparing meals for training days. Thinking outside of the box allowed more volunteers to be a part of what God was doing in children's ministry while freeing my time so I could serve volunteers better.

HOW CAN YOU START BUILDING A TEAM?

So far I've written about where volunteers come from and how to serve them, but how do you go about building a team? How this looks and what challenges come up will differ for each church, but the steps listed below will be the same whether you have an existing team or are starting from scratch. I have also provided questions to help you self-reflect as you plan.

Prepare with prayer. Building a team begins and continues with *you!* Jesus took time in solitude and prayer as he prepared for the tasks God had for him. He understood the importance of being near to God to stay in tune to God's calling on his life. Are you following in his example? Privately answer these questions: When was the last time you asked God to prepare you to be the leader he is calling you to be? Have you asked God to show you areas you need to grow in? Have you asked God to help you lead with grace and humility? Your response to these questions may indicate a need to focus your heart toward God's call in your life.

Establish clear vision and values. Is your vision simple and easy to follow? What culture is being modeled through your values, and does it need to change? If you are part of a church plant, you are blessed to be able to create the culture you desire from the beginning. However, it is important to plan and communicate with the lead pastor so that the culture you are creating aligns with the vision and culture of the church. Changing the culture in an established church can be difficult and will take time and grace on your part. You will find that you will start losing volunteers, and that is scary. What I found, however, is the people who stepped down were the volunteers who needed to be removed because they were hindering the ministry. Once more people heard about the vision and culture that was being set, I noticed that more top-quality volunteers jumped at the opportunity to be a part of what God was doing. Quality volunteers will choose to follow strong leaders; strong leaders make healthy changes that will grow God's kingdom instead of pushing for their own personal projects or preferences! Ask yourself:

- What vision and values are leading your ministry and does it support the overall vision and culture for the church?
- Is your vision simple and easy to understand and memorize?
- Do you have three to seven core values to set the culture of your ministry?

Create a plan. Once you have your vision and values you'll need to come up with a plan or strategy. This will help you communicate how you plan to accomplish your vision and values so your volunteers know what's expected, where your ministry is going, and how to get to the end goal. Part of planning is making sure your curriculum, activities, and ministry events align with your vision and values. Whatever does not support those is not going to help you accomplish your goals. You will need to decide what is worth saving and what needs to be dropped. For example, the children's ministry team I led put on a family movie night twice a year. The movie night was meant to be a fun and safe place to bring family and friends. The environment fit into our values, but it was missing a key element of our vision: "experiencing God together." As a team, we decided to gear the event to make it a "fun and safe place to bring family and friends" where they could "experience God in a non-threatening way."

As the leader you are going to face hard decisions. When difficult choices surface, ask yourself if they are going to propel your vision forward or just clutter up the calendar. Ask yourself these questions as you begin to formulate a plan:

- What are your ministry policies and expectations? These provide safety and clear expectations for volunteers and children.

- How are the classes or kids' services going to flow? (Routines, service orders, etc.)?
- How are you going to recruit, train, and develop your team?
- How many volunteers are needed, and how are you going to schedule them? (Great tool for scheduling: planningcenteronline.com)
- Have you created an annual calendar (events for ministry and team, trainings, personal prayer and dream-casting days, ministry emphasis days [videos, bulletin, stage time, etc.])?
- What are you going to use for curriculum, or how are you going to put together a lesson plan?
- How are you going to decorate to create a welcoming and kid-friendly environment?

Recruit and train volunteers. This is an area that you cannot check off your to-do list. Recruiting is one of the hardest parts of your job, but you don't have to do it alone. Your other volunteers are a great resource to help recruit new people, but you have to build that into the culture of your team. You will need to encourage your team to be recruiters. One way to build this into your team is to give opportunities for volunteers to share stories about what God is doing in their lives and the lives of others. Stories get people talking, and word of mouth is one of the best ways to draw in new volunteers. Another way to recruit volunteers is to make yourself available in the lobby or coffee shop of your church. This allows you to share life with others and build relationships. As you invest in others you will learn about their gifts and passions, and that is a great way to find your teachers, assistants, greeters, prayer partners, and organizers.

Once you've recruited volunteers, take them through a screening process. Have the individuals fill out an application, check references, do a background check, and have the person come in and share his or her story. Have a few questions ready that will help you identify whether or not the individual will be a good fit for the values and culture of your ministry. This is also a great time to allow the person to ask questions about the ministry.

After the screening process is complete, train your volunteers! Don't just throw them in the deep end of the pool and expect them to succeed. Teach them about the expectations, allow them to observe, and put them under stronger team member who can model the culture and train them well. Ask yourself:

- What's your plan? (Remember to think outside the box.)
- Are you making yourself available to people?
- Who are your key volunteers who can help train others?

Build up a core team. Jesus taught the masses, but he chose a select few to invest in and mentor. He spent time teaching, praying with, and serving them. He empowered them to share the gospel and apprentice others. As a leader, you need to find a select few that you can invest in, train, and develop into leaders who will follow your example and apprentice others.

As you choose those key leaders, remember the importance of having a diverse group of volunteers. Look for volunteers who are strong in areas in which you are weak. Empower them to do what you can't. Involve others who may think differently than you. Your way is not always the best; you need people that can see things you cannot and are confident enough to speak up in a respectful way.

In the book *Decisive: How to Make Better Choices in Life and Work*, Chip Heath and Dan Heath write about the importance of considering opposing views. They are speaking of CEOs who overpay for acquisitions due to their own "exaggerated pride or self confidence."[52] One way the authors talk about overcoming such hubris is to consider different views when making important decisions. The Heath brothers write, "Few of us are stuck in a bubble of power like a CEO, and our hubris levels are mercifully lower, but we do have something in common with them: a bias to favor our own beliefs. Our 'bubble' is not the boardroom, it's the brain."[53]

Chances are you are not a CEO of a large corporation, but this same principle applies in children's ministry. Each person's opinions and thoughts can put him or her in a bubble and keep the individual from growing into a better leader. That is why having a diverse group of volunteers is essential. I never want my own limited thoughts and opinions to cripple me or others.

- What five to ten volunteers can you invest in and train up?
- How are you going to mentor them?
- What areas can you give others ownership in?
- Are you allowing others (especially those who are different from you) to share their opinions and ideas?

Model Christ and serve your team. Jesus didn't lead by telling his disciples what to do; he modeled it for them, showing them how to serve and love others. I love the story in John 13:1–17 where we see Jesus washing the disciples' feet, modeling his love and selfless, serving attitude. Then he calls them to follow his example, saying: "Now that I, your Lord and Teacher, have washed your feet, you also should wash one another's feet. I have set you an example that you should do as I have done for you" (John 13:14–15, NIV). What an amazing role model to follow! Show your team what servanthood means and invite them into this same type of servant life; it will drastically change the culture of your team. Ask yourself:

- What can I continue to learn from Jesus' example?
- In what way can I lead by selflessly serving without expecting anything in return?
- Am I living out the expectations and values I ask of your volunteers? If not, how can I change that?

You can now rest assured knowing that reading this has officially made you an expert at working with volunteers. (Just kidding! Working with volunteers is something you'll become better at over time, with experience and continual learning.) As you grow and develop yourself and your team, lean on God for wisdom and guidance. Follow the example he set in Christ by serving and loving your volunteers. Remember that God is your biggest fan! He has chosen and empowered you to lead his people, and "[he] who calls you is faithful, and he will do it" (1 Thessalonians 5:24, NIV).

Dream big!

REFLECTION QUESTIONS

1. What are three different recruiting techniques you can use to get more people involved?

2. What are five ways you can serve your volunteers so that they know they are valued and important?

3. What is your strategy to clearly communicate the vision, values, and expectations to your volunteers?

4. What culture are you setting through your example right now?

5. Does the culture need to change? If so, how can you change it?

PART THREE: ENVIRONMENT

Environment describes the condition or surroundings in which we livew it is just about everything. The ability to create an effective environment in your church is critical. Great content often gets lost in a shabby presentation. Kids learn in multiF sensory ways and we must learn how to speak their language. This section is huge and we have some great ideas for you to consider.

Craig Geis starts by describing "The Value of Environment." We see how building environments is more than "looking cool" and makes powerful connections with your kids and families. Lauren Beach talks about "Hitting Your Target Audience" and helps you figure out who you are talking to. Finally, Sam Korslund rocks a discussion on "Checking In" and describes the centrality of your church check in/out system.

3.1- THE VALUE OF ENVIRONMENT
Craig Geis

MORE THAN "LOOKING COOL"

What is the value of an environment? The old adage in business used to be "location, location, location." If you had the right location, it would not matter what you offered to the community, it would sell. Today location is less compelling compared to *what* is offered and *how*.

However, a compelling environment is essential to fulfilling Christ's mission to make and teach disciples. It's not enough to be easy to find, we must also be interesting to find. The attractive qualities of a kid's area will help bring families back time and time again. Those of us who minister to children see the value of environment right off the bat. It deserves our attention and contributes to the effectiveness of our ministries far beyond "looking cool."

There are three key elements that should be addressed in a children's ministry environment and we are going to talk about them. The next few pages will focus on why an environment is important to children and their families, what makes up an environment, and how to create an environment while keeping it within your budget. Our goal here is not to provide all of the answers, but help you consider your own environments and how you can take them to the next level. In case you are not yet convinced, let's start by addressing the most important question: *why*?

WHY ENVIRONMENT?

Why is it necessary to have a space that appeals to kids? Answering that question sheds light on the needs of children and their different modes of learning. It is easy to see that children growing up in small churches decades ago would have sat with their parents in a single service that was mainly for adult audiences. Children were hushed for loud voices, told to pay attention, and sit up straight. There may have been a short message for the children, but after it was back to the regular service. Imagine going to a church gathering and learning about Jesus but not being able to read about him or study his word. Roll back our timeline to a bit earlier and see that same child working six days a week. In the eighteenth-century England, a poor kid's only opportunity to learn might have been at a new event called, "Sunday school." This revolutionary form of education began to take shape in the 1780s in Britain. This was birthed from the heart of Robert Raikes, an English Anglican evangelical.[54] Raikes felt that literacy could liberate an entire generation from poverty. This model of public child education would evolve into the types of elementary schools that we recognize today. This example of the need for learning among children does not stop with language, mathematics, and economics. It continues with a focus on education that is suited to age groups and learning styles.

If you enter a school classroom today, you would be able to figure out which age of kid the classroom is designed for. You would know by the height of the desks or by the type of decorations that adorn the wall. Age-appropriate learning spaces are essential to educators; they should be essential for us as well.

The ability to learn is a gift from God and the environment of learning can be controlled by people, space, and learning items. Just as adults would be uncomfortable having a class in a nursery, surrounded by toys and cribs, so are children when they do not have an age-appropriate space in which to learn. Children tend to connect with others and retain more information when they feel welcome and safe. Material and messages designed for children engage them and draw them in so they can have the opportunity to continue learning about Jesus.

Some would argue that keeping the children with them during service helps to unify the body of Christ. That is a valid point. When the body stays in one room they are together; however, they may not be unified in Christ as much as they are simply unified in church. From personal experience, I learned how to play quietly with my toys in my pew. I was not learning very much. When I was asked about my action figures and what I was playing, with guns quietly firing, I would stop and reply with a lie, "They are going to church!" I also learned how to go to sleep during the service without causing too much attention. The Sunday night service turned out to be a great place for a five-year-old to "rest" in the Lord. This can be true today. Most children who attend adult services, in adult environments, tend to check out. They play quietly, study the maps in the backs of Bibles, or zone into their parent's smart phone. There is nothing wrong with churches beginning with everyone worshiping together before dismissing to classes meant for them. This could be the best of both worlds when it comes to wanting children with families and at the same time the ability to have children taught at their level and their peers. Regardless of how your church approaches the idea of families attending church together, we can agree that people learn best in environments suited for them.

Parents today are more likely to choose a church based on the experience of their kids. Involvement in extracurricular programs has burgeoned in the past twenty years. Children are busier than ever and the competition for their free time has never been fiercer. If you want the family then you have to win over the whole family. Remember that parents can see how much you value their kids. Every poster, classroom door, and sign says something about your ministry. All of these factors have significantly raised the bar when it comes to making kids feel welcome.

What Makes an Environment?

According to Webster, one's environment includes "the conditions that surround someone or something: the conditions and influences that affect the growth, health, progress, etc., of someone or something." Consider what elements make up your environment and how those elements are employed. Each stapler, table, song, or light fixture will serve to help—or hurt—the discipleship process in your church. More importantly, the way in which you use each of these elements is critical. You don't have to have "all the right stuff" to teach kids. But you do have to have the right attitude. The conditions of an environment can lead to positive or negative growth, health, and progress within the age group. Let us start with a look at the nursery area.

Babies are horrible at memorizing Scripture; they just are. Besides having poor penmanship many of them are lazy and just sit around all day. This is why early childhood environments will be less about education and more about creating a safe place, which is communicated through the five senses of touch, taste, smell, hearing, and sight. This should be a crucial consideration when painting or equipping any area. For example when I first joined the staff of our church, our baby nursery had a mural of children painted on the wall. The mural portrayed children playing, but unfortunately the eyes of the children had been scratched out. The primary colors used did not help the situation either. The carpet had no padding and was glued directly to concrete. There were two old, wooden rocking chairs, a few toys, and three stacked, chicken-coop-style cribs. The space was run-down, cold, and uninviting. When my wife began watching babies in the nursery she asked for some new paint and some other comforts for the space. We came up with a design change that included plush carpet, neutral-colored paint, some new used toys, and two donated Pack'N Plays. The idea was to bring a living room into the nursery, so the baby would feel more at home and less as if in a gulag. The carpet and padding helped to dampen echoes in the room and helped the room feel warm; parents loved how squishy the carpet felt when they brought their babies into the nursery. This helped create an environment for babies that would lead to fewer head bonks on the floor, and we also noticed caregivers sliding onto the floor to interact with the babies. With happier caregivers and a comfortable space, the babies had the opportunity to enjoy their church experience, which would then lead to being able to learn more about Christ as they became older.

My wife reminded me recently of how this can feel for a child. While she was attending a different church for a women's Bible study, she used to drop our then-two-year-old off with caregivers. Our son, now eighteen, told her that he remembers going down a dark hallway with the caregiver and that it made him uncomfortable. I believe him, because discomfort can be observed in the eyes and actions of children when they come into an environment that is unknown to them.

In order for lives to be changed by God's Word, obstacles that make children uncomfortable should be removed or minimized at all costs. Each age group's space or classroom should be set up to enhance the experience and keep from detracting from the message.

Whether you are looking at making a space for babies, preschoolers or elementary students, at times it will be necessary to review and evaluate how the space is functioning and if there should be adjustments. At times you will have a group that requires a certain sized room, and it can be a problem if the right-sized room has been decorated or structurally set up for different age group. Your environment should be flexible enough to receive whatever group needs the space when the size of the space determines the group. If you have the resources and time to change rooms to fit the ages, go for it! If your church is like many others, you might need to think about having multi-functional rooms with items and decorations that can be changed to match the current age group.

Other factors involving the function and layout of a space should be taken into consideration in order to ensure the best use of the space. Things to think about include: the temperature, the smell, the accessibility, the touch factor, the playability, the cleanliness, the colors, and the people that will be teaching the children. The temperature needs to be comfortable for the time of year, which means you may have to look into heaters, air conditioners, or other facility improvements. The space must smell clean and be clean. If your space allows for it, try to have your children's classes as close together as possible, for the sake of security. Security brings peace to families delivering children, and the children can sense it.

Take a look at your facility through the eyes of a child and make notes for adjustment. If necessary, invite someone that has not been to your facility before to help evaluate hidden flaws. When going through the spaces remember to check for the five-sense impact of smell, touch, sight, sound, and taste (i.e., snacks).

Finally, the people that you put in front of the children have a lot to do with how the children will feel about their visit or attendance at your church. This is the most critical part of any successful environment: getting the right people on board. With the right leader or teacher, you could meet in a hallway or a small blank room and the children will be transported to Egypt anyway, crossing the Red Sea with the children of Israel. The right leader or teacher will be able involve the kids in games and stories that can keep them engaged for the entire time. The environment becomes less important to the kids when their teachers are good. At our church we have minimal decorations on walls and I encourage team teachers to interact and engage with the kids as much as possible.

With all considerations of environment, the biggest difficulty will be money. But whether you have some or none, there is always hope for great spaces at your church.

No Money, Mo' Problems?

Environments can get as elaborate as California theme parks or they can occupy a single corner of a room. They can cost hundreds of thousands of dollars or be made up of things donated and recycled. Dreams cost nothing, but remodeling or bringing in amazing 3D structures can cost quite a lot. Let's look at creating an environment without a lot of money.

Consider the tone of your church before you start creating new children's ministry spaces. Factors relating to your city, the type of people who attend your church, and current aesthetics should factor in. Does a nautical theme fit best on the Pacific coast or in the Kansas sun? What are your parents looking for in a facility? Does your school district consist of brand new buildings or old ones? Do members of the congregation live in old or new housing developments? Has your church committed to existing decorating themes already? With answers to these types of questions, you can begin to frame the theme and decorations you want to work toward obtaining or creating.

My church exists in an urban neighborhood, and I was inspired by the color of nearby college apartments. I made some space to have a playroom behind a check-in counter that had doors from the playroom into various preschool classrooms. Outdoor playground equipment came inside, placed on top of green remnant carpet that represented grass. The doors to the classes were altered to look like doors to various connected buildings. Indoor and outdoor panel boards provided the textures I wanted and the colors were made similar to the apartments. In front of building fronts, I laid a strip of grey remnant carpet to represent the sidewalk. Brick panel board became the front of the check-in counter—and the Kid City Park came into being.

Paint is an inexpensive and easy way to change the look of a space, particularly in older buildings. From a fresh coat of paint to a piece of art that you and a friend sketch on with a video projector, you can create a stir and interest easily. Mobile children's ministries can employ the same technique by using 4x8 sheets of wood or PVC-framed canvas to carry a portable image. The name of your ministry can go on a wall or mobile piece quite easily and adds to the décor. Posted Scripture verses can help accentuate the things you value, such as the beatitudes, the fruit of the spirit, or the armor of God. These postings can be referred to on a regular basis and could take the place of class rules.

Painting walls can feel somewhat permanent, but curriculum themes and ministry names change often. A suggestion would be to use posters and decorations that can be changed out at least quarterly. This is all to keep things fresh and keep the kids interested in their surroundings. You could involve kids by having them bring some of the decorations that will be placed on display (with their parents' permission, of course). Decorations that are interactive would be a great way to exercise some of their senses in relation to their environment. Using the natural tree limbs, leaves, cactus, or whatever natural decorations you find can enhance your theme and stir interest. Involve children in painting projects in whatever capacity you feel comfortable with. They could paint leaves, handprints, or possibly memory verse posters that could be laminated to use and then reuse at a later date.

Recycling is something that is being done all over the world, but how can we connect that with lost-cost environments? A number of walls were torn down as we laid the foundation for my Kid City Playground. The lumber was removed carefully so it could be used later. A large room needed to be divided into two rooms by an accordion door, which we salvaged from another room in the church. All the carpet that was installed was remnants, which meant adjusting for color, texture, and availability. It pays to be flexible which will save you money in the long run. If you have a dream but your budget will not fit your space the consider augmenting the dream! Another way to get the job done is to hold your desires loosely while hanging on to the overall vision. Watch TV shows that show you how to repurpose low-cost items. Use old curtains to divide big spaces into smaller spaces for small groups and activity stations. Our use of recycled and repurposed materials took a $48,000 project down $24,000.

Creating a great space for kids is time-consuming, and energy-draining, but it's worth it to reap the reward of their pleased reactions to the changes. They will see love in action and know that they are cared for enough to have improvements made to their learning space. Do whatever it takes to make a place for the children of your church excited to invite their friends to.

REFLECTION QUESTIONS

1. What would it take to develop an environment that is age-appropriate and that would fit in the framework of your churches ministry?

2. Safety is an aspect of the environment that must be addressed. Could your security improve?

3. Would you describe your children's ministry Bible teaching as "creative"? How can you change the method without changing the message?

4. Is "fun" currently part of your ministry to children? How could you implement fun that is also instructional?

5. How can you incorporate the five senses into your children's ministry?

3.2 - HITTING YOUR TARGET AUDIENCE
Lauren Beach

SINK OR SWIM WITH A RUBBER CHICKEN

How many times have you taught a lesson, and walked away saying to yourself, "I don't know if anyone was picking up what I was putting down." The constant flow of bathroom requests, yawns, and misbehavior don't install a lot of confidence for those up front. It's tough to guarantee that each child will experience some sort of lifeF change on a weekly basis. However, it is our job as the teacher, the leader, the shepherd of these children, to do our part in teaching kids about Jesus. When preparing a lesson for kids, we must learn how to define, and reach a target audience. This chapter we will examine why a target audience is important, what types of young disciples you are likely to encounter, and why small groups for kids are important. Each of these will play into how you will write and present your lessons.

I remember one of my first experiences teaching kids at church. I was a college student at Northwest University and was tackling one of my first assignments in a course called "Communicating with Children." I realized I had never actually taught to a group of kids before. I was terrified. I thought they would eat me alive, or worse—that they would say that I was boring! I started to panic. The children's pastor I was serving under came up with the perfect solution. He told me I was going to teach to a boys' group that night. I started freaking out, and didn't know what to say, or what they would understand. For the first time, I gathered my thoughts, rolled up my sleeves, and reached for a rubber chicken. Let me tell you, my lesson wasn't anything spectacular. I might have stumbled through one of Jesus' own stories about seeds, and soil, and rubber chickens; the facts are still a bit blurry. But I learned a lot through this experience. The only way to get good at teaching kids is *to teach kids!*

When we are speaking to anyone the first thing we need to do is determine who our target audience is. A target audience may be defined as *an intended group for which something is performed or marketed; the specific group to which advertising is directed.*

As you sit down to gather your notes be sure to answer the following questions: Why am I teaching this lesson? Why am I doing what I'm doing? Why does this matter to the audience and why does your audience matter to you? You need to start by setting some goals. Create goals that define what the kids should learn from the lesson. These goals will naturally occur once you define the why.

WHO IS YOUR AUDIENCE?

When you are thinking of teaching kids you need to understand who is in your audience. First, determine the age of the kids being taught. Everyone knows that teaching to a mixed group that ranges from preschoolers to fifth-graders is crazy. Teaching a first-grader and a fourth-grader is equally difficult. I taught the story of Noah in one such class, and when I asked the kids what types of birds Noah released from the ark, one talkative first-grade boy's hand shot up, so I called on him. He proudly answered the question, "a glove and a raisin." Glove/dove, raisin/raven—

close enough! This first-grader was trying to pay attention and trying to understand two types of birds he had never heard of before. The older kids giggled and rolled their eyes; they would have never made such a mistake. This experience helped me understand the different educational stages of elementary-aged kids.

When you are teaching to a specific audience you need to keep in mind where the kids are developmentally as well as what type of kids you are speaking to. Consider this brief description of each of the stages of learning.

Early childhood: Ages 2–7. Children at this age starting to realize who they are, which leads them into a egocentric world that is all about *me*. They have vivid imaginations and they naturally imitate the adults in their lives. The children in this stage are forever impacted by stories, examples, and the faith that they see in the adults in their lives. These children are trying to act like adults, so the adults in their lives must be authentic. At this stage, children are coming to the awareness that they exist and that God exists as well.

Childhood: Ages 8–11. In this stage a child learns more about concrete operational thinking. This means that they are starting to think and talk about their actions. They have the ability to prolong activities and reverse actions that they were unable to do when they were younger. They move away from their pretending stage and move toward wanting to figure out how to interact with other children around them. James Fowler calls this "Mythical-literal Faith."[55] During this stage a child's relationship with Jesus is explored and they begin to ask questions in order to find out more about who he is. They are starting to be able to connect with the stories they hear to see if they apply to their lives.

Adolescence: Ages 13–21. This stage is marked with an increased amount of focus, capacity, and stability. Adolescents can logically solve problems and can explain how they came to their conclusions. These young adults are beginning to develop their own unique identity and role in the world. During this stage students start asking questions on how things relate to them and they start striving to find the answers to those questions. During this time is usually when young people start to take their faith as their own.

These are just brief descriptions of how each age group learns, processes information, and comes to faith. For more information, read the book, *The Seven Laws of the Learner.*[56]

After you learn about the ones you are targeting, you must also realize that each kid in your group learns differently. There are three general modes of perceiving ideas: audible, visual, and kinesthetic. Audio learners absorb best by listening to people. Visual learners need to see pictures, examples, and how things connect. The kinesthetic learner does best by touch, feeling, being a part of what is going on. Studies have shown that classes will learn the most when the teacher uses all three learning styles together. So when you are targeting a class, you must think about who is in the audience and then see how you can add in pieces of each of these learning styles.

That was a whirlwind summary! Yet we are not quite done.

TARGETED LEARNING AND THE DISCOVERY PROCESS

Two words: small groups. In know, in order to have small groups we will need to have tons of volunteers, and small groups can take tons of time. Yet I believe that small groups are one of the most important things that we can do with our time. Why? Because, when you add small groups to your children's ministry, kids have the opportunity to develop relationships with other kids as well as relationships with their leader. When there is a real relationship, kids are more willing to talk about what is going on in their lives and ask the questions that they may have. In addition, leaders will have the chance to get to know each of the kids. In a word, in small groups, kids will have the ability to discover God's truth within a group of like-minded peers.

In a large group setting, it is often very difficult to teach both first and sixth-graders. The application for each of these groups may be very different and difficult to pull together. This is why you must to choose a target audience before dismissing the kids into small groups. The small group environment is where team leaders personalize the lesson for each individual age group. Within these groups you can go as deep or as slow as you need for the age of the kids in your group. When you have these groups, try not to just give the kids yes or no questions, but challenge them with open-ended questions that get them thinking. Something happens in the kids when they are able to sit down listen to a lesson, and then have the opportunity to process it out loud in their small groups. You will notice a change in your kids and also your leaders. If you are not doing small groups already, I would recommend splitting the kids into age groups. (If you are living dangerously, you can also split these age groups up by gender.)

WRAPPING IT UP

Teaching kids is such a wonderful privilege. They are teachable and looking to learn and understand what is going on around them. So in short, we need to be prepared for whatever challenges that we meet. We need to remember why it is important to target a specific group or audience, and where your kids are developmentally as well as spiritually. I challenge you to try using each of the three different learning styles throughout your lesson. Yes, this will be tough, but it is important! When you do this you might be surprised on what happens to the kids in your ministry.

Remember that you are not ever doing this alone; God can use your message to speak to any child, right where they are. When we target who we are speaking to, we are giving the Holy Spirit more opportunities to work in kids' lives.

REFLECTION QUESTIONS

1.   How do you prepare to speak to kids with different learning styles
      and at different stages of faith?
2.   What is the best way for kids to discover God's truth in your Sunday
      gathering? What things can you do to help them consider the right
      type of questions?
3.   How can you prepare your volunteers to identify different types of
      learners? How do they understand different age groups, learning
      styles, or maturity of faith?

3.3 - CHECKING IN
Sam Korslund

OF MONSTERS AND MICE

Let me start this chapter with something near and dear to my heart: monster trucks. I am unashamed in my love of massively overF powered machines making an obscene amount of noise while jumping, crushing, spinning, and wrecking. Of course, as any father would, I wanted to share this love of mine with my two boys. So a couple years ago my wife and I took them to their first monster truck show.

I had purchased the tickets online and had to pick them up at the arena. After waiting quite a while in line, I arrived at the willF call booth with my ID and receipt for the tickets in hand, ready to receive my tickets. The attendant, however, just asked for my last name and handed the tickets right over without even asking if I had any proof that I was who I said I was, or that I had purchased the tickets being given to me. This also left me wondering, why was the line moving so slowly if all they were doing was handing tickets out based on a corresponding last name?

We proceeded to the entry gate, had our tickets scanned and were allowed inside the building. Once inside, we were left to our own devices to navigate the arena, find the correct section, row, and seats, and to enjoy the spectacle and awe of watching ridiculously jacked-up trucks burning fossil fuels while crushing old junkers. The boys and I loved it. My wife was just glad she remembered her earplugs.

Following the show, it was bedlam trying to find the right exit. We carefully made our way through the crowds, each keeping a hand on at least one of our kids to make sure we all stayed together. Then, for reasons that I can't even comprehend now (but I'm assuming I must have breathed in too much truck exhaust), we decided that we hadn't had enough of crowds, loud noises, and excitement, so we decided to take our boys somewhere special for dinner. We went to Chuck E. Cheese of all places.

As we pulled into the mouse themed restaurant, the excitement in our boys grew to a fever pitch. Once the doors opened the sights, the sounds, even the smells were more than they could stand. Upon reaching the front of the line, which didn't take long at all, we were greeted by a friendly person who welcomed us and checked us in. We all received a hand stamp that was unique to our family. Signs pointed us towards restrooms, activities, and eating areas. Lights highlighted the things they wanted us to see and employees wandered the spaces offering help and directions.

The reason I'm sharing this story is to illustrate two very different experiences my family had upon entering two different facilities. "Inefficient," "slow, and "insecure" describe the arena experience, while "quick," "intentional and "friendly" describe our Chuck E. Cheese's experience. Allow me to pivot to a third environment: your children experiences my family had amp that only our family would have, which we could smells were almost more than they could stand's is with the children being entrusted to us? Most parents will only experience your children the children being entrust their kids in and out. So answer this: What does their experience say about your ministry? Are you more like a monster truck or a mouse?

WHY SHOULD I?

Not everyone reading this may use a check-in system in their kids' ministry, or even think it is necessary. Because of that, before detailing the environment of a check-in process and how it can impact your ministry, I first want to address those of you who may not be using one.

On just about every event ticket I've ever seen there is a common disclaimer stating the facility, performers, and anyone else associated with the event is not responsible for any injury, loss, theft, blah, blah, blah. They want to limit their liability should anything unpleasant occur with someone attending that event. I'm also fairly certain that limiting liabilities for the corporation plays pretty heavily into Chuck E. Cheese's emphasis on the check-in/check-out system at their restaurants.

We all know that we live in a society inundated with a "sue first, ask questions later" mentality, so what I'm about to write may come as a surprise. There are only two reasons why a kids' ministry should use a check-in system, and neither of them has anything to do with limiting our liability.

TOO BIG, TOO SMALL, JUST RIGHT

When it comes to using a check-in/check-out system in kids' ministry, it is first and foremost about the safety of the kids. We live in a broken world where some people are willing to hurt children. It is our responsibility to put up as many roadblocks as we can to protect those who have been entrusted to us.

None of us, whether from a big city or small town, megachurch, or country chapel, want to believe that anything bad could ever happen to us.

Even so, it would be naïve of us to assume that we are exempt from danger. With that in mind we have to remain diligent in using whatever methods possible to protect our kids.

In today's world we also have more blended families than ever before. We have to realize that we don't know every family dynamic and custody arrangement, taking for granted that it's OK if a parent may attempt to pick their child up from our ministry unbeknownst to the other parent. It is critical to the safety of the child to be able to verify that the parent trying to pick them up did not drop them off, and being able to contact the other parent.

Again, none of us ever wants to imagine these situations happening anywhere, let alone at our church, in our ministry, to our kids. However, our assumptions on the likelihood of a situation like this never happening do not absolve us of our responsibility to be prepared for it.

It Isn't About You

The second reason why a kids' ministry should be using a check-in system is for parents, and by that I mean parents who are new to your church and ministry. When we first implemented a check-in system at our church, we received a fair amount of pushback from the parents of kids who had been part of the kids' ministry for a while. They were wondering why we needed to go through the hassle when we only had about twenty kids at that time. We all knew the kids, their families, who came with whom and who was supposed to leave with whom. My response to them was a kind and gentle way of saying, "this isn't about you."

To explain what I mean by that, let's go back to Chuck E. Cheese's. When my wife and I took our boys there, it was complete, total chaos. With all the kids running every direction, the noise, the lights, the crowd—it was overwhelming. We were still playing with our kids and we kept them close to us, but we were able to relax a little bit knowing that there was a secure system in place for their safety. If for some reason, we couldn't immediately spot our kids in the crowd we didn't have to wonder if they were still in the building or not. We knew they would be where we would be able to find them.

When a new family arrives at your church, they are already uneasy. Even if they have been attending church elsewhere, they are now walking out of their comfort zone into a new culture they don't know, filled with people they don't know. Once they find the kids' ministry location, they are then about to trust their most prized possessions—their children—into the hands of complete strangers. Put yourself in their shoes. Wouldn't you feel more at ease knowing that the people in your church take that trust at least as seriously as Chuck E. Cheese?

THE CHECK-IN ENVIRONMENT

The environment for a check-in area consists of three basic things: the check-in system, the physical space, and the people. Each of these provides a critical portion of the first impression new parents will have of your ministry. And remember, most parents won't see much of what happens during kids' church so most of what forms their opinions of your ministry is what they see for themselves, namely, the check-in and check-out process.

THE SYSTEM

Your check-in system doesn't have to be expensive. Our conversation is going to focus on digital solutions but know that there are many other ways of establishing a clear and secure check-in/check-out system. Paper tickets, stickers, and laminated cards are a few ways that you can start with little money down. The truth is that many digital solutions today are extremely affordable. Before you get out the scissors and hole-punch, spend some time online. These programs range from one-time cost to monthly subscription-based systems. Any of these would likely do everything you would need to implement a check-in system, and lots more. But don't get stuck in thinking you need to buy one of these systems. In our modern tech-savvy society, pen and paper both still work, and will accomplish the goal of checking kids into and out of your ministry. My emphatic point is if you are not currently doing anything, *do something!*

I firmly believe the advantages provided by a digital system make it worthwhile to invest in, but that still doesn't mean you need to buy or subscribe to some expensive software. The check-in system we use was designed by a church member with an engineering background. It is customized to provide all the functionality we need, all for the one-time cost of the base software used to create it. Maybe you have someone in your church who is a capable computer programmer. Share the vision with that person—what you are wanting, and why—and you may be able to get a custom system for your ministry at a very low cost. Whatever your system, whether you use a pen, a mouse, or a stylus, it must be secure, reliable, quick, and effective.

Secure. Remember the number one reason you have a check-in system is *safety*. A check-in system will obviously need to list the names of children and their parents. Beyond that, a digital system will also likely contain personal information, such as home and email addresses and phone numbers, all of which need to be kept secure. Digital systems have the advantage of passwords and security locks to keep that information private and available to only those who need to access it.

Reliable. No matter how many times you perfectly set up prior to a service, something will go wrong. We've all experienced those times when everything is cruising along perfectly and the projector goes down, the microphones stop working, the guitar breaks a string, or a volunteer doesn't show up. If you are looking for a system, read the customer reviews. Ask other churches what they use. What are their volunteers saying about it? Does it crash or lock up? Does it do what it is supposed to do? If you're using a digital system, how old is the computer that is running it? If you like a web-based system, how reliable and fast is your Internet connection? One thing to consider on a Web-based system is people coming to your church and connecting to the church's Wi-Fi. The more devices connected, the slower your connection speed can become, which could create problems for a Web-based check-in system.

Quick. If your church is anything like ours, you can count on a rush of families showing up just before the service starts to check their kids in. The last thing you need is a bottleneck at your check-in station. While this does afford the opportunity to connect with the parents, no one wants to wait in long lines to check their kids in before making their way to the adult gathering. Whatever system you choose it should handle the check-in portion quickly and efficiently. Certain functions, such as adding a new family, will take a bit more time and there are ways to speed that up while still checking other kids in. This could mean more than one station operating simultaneously, or a separate way of gathering that newcomer data.

For instance, at our church we have what we call Connection Cards. These are cards that newcomers can use to give us their names, kids' names and ages, contact information, and request information on various ministries. I've started keeping a stack of those cards at our check-in desk and when a new family arrives, we simply ask them to complete the card. This gives us an opportunity to connect with them while still getting all the information we need for our check-in system, and allows us to continue checking other kids in while getting that information.

Effective. The bottom line for whatever system you use: it needs to be effective. Does your system accomplish the goal of securely checking kids into and out of your kids' ministry? If not, what needs to change about it?

The space. No facility is perfect. Some churches have the luxury of a purpose-built kids' wing, while others are using a couple classrooms at the end of the hall. Check-in could happen in a kid's foyer or at the door to individual rooms, either way the space being used contributes to the overall environment of your check-in system.

The physical space you use should allow for a few things. First, it needs to be in a location where the families need to go in order to get to your kids' ministry. In other words, check-in should be happening at the main entrance, not off in the corner or at the back of the room. This can be a challenge if you have multiple entry points to the area where kids' ministry happens, but try to find the best area to position the check-in where you can see who is coming and going, and where they can see you as well.

Hopefully you have enough space for a few families to gather. Again, no facility is perfect, and this may seem impossible, but families need to be able to enter at the same time other parents are leaving to attend the adult gathering. This will also give enough room for some members of your kids' staff to be there to connect with the parents, give them any updates or information you may have, and give them an opportunity to share with you anything that may be happening with their child that morning.

Going beyond simple square footage, what does the space say about your ministry? Is it bright, fun and engaging? How is it decorated? Are there printed materials like kids' ministry brochures or bulletins available for newcomers? Not that anyone is probably going to accept Jesus as Lord based on the décor of your check-in area, but this is another way to engage with your parents and demonstrate to them that you are intentional in all areas of the ministry that you provide for the spiritual growth of their child.

The people. The final and most important contributor to the check-in environment is the people you have running the system and connecting with the parents. No amount of space, computer programming, decorating or planning can come close to the impact your people can have on your parents. The people you want out there should have a very special skill set, but they may not be the skills you would automatically assume.

One common mistake is to think that if you are using a digital check-in that you need someone that is pretty tech-savvy to run it. Most of these systems are fairly basic to operate by design. The companies that make them design their systems for a wide variety of people to be able to use them, so they have to make the process simple, straightforward and easy to learn.

By far, the most important personal qualities that significantly impact the environment of your check-in area are the ability to put a name to a face, and to do so with a smile. Several years ago, when I had first decided I would check out that whole "church thing," we made the decision on which one to attend based on the fact that the people would remember our name by the second time we went. That's it. It really was that simple. The people at the church where we ended up were friendly, welcoming, and they remembered all of our names. We were no longer those anonymous newbies; we felt like part of the family. We felt like we belonged. Never underestimate the impact that remembering a name from one week to the next will have on a newcomer. If you can find a few people who can do that, and do it with a smile on their faces, you will be able to recoup any amount of training you have to invest in order to bring them up to speed on running the system.

Another mistake is thinking that all you really need is one person in the area to check people in. That is obviously a good start, but you should have at least one other person out in the area to be a connection point for your parents and the kids. This person could hand out information on an upcoming event, complement a little girl on her dress, give high-fives, direct people to the appropriate spaces, and meet the newcomers as they arrive. This was one of many things I overlooked when we began using a check-in system.

We had one person in the check-in area who was trying to do it all, and of course it was too much for one person to do. When we added that additional connection person I began to notice that the communication with parents improved and newcomers were getting better connected on that first visit. The whole process just got better by leaps and bounds. Kids were even coming in with bigger smiles because someone had greeted them by name, asked them about their football game, complimented them on their outfit. Basically, someone took the time to show them they care about them before they even got in the doors of the kids' church.

BEYOND CHUCK E. CHEESE'S

Keep these two big ideas in focus: you want kids to be safe, and you want visitors to leave feeling that they can trust you with their kids.

There are numerous additional benefits to be realized through the use of a system. Check-in systems provide an open environment where parents can engage with members of your team. Newcomers connect with your ministry. Kids are greeted and welcomed, and families feel safe and secure. These are all reasons to intentionally create an environment where these things happen.

Don't get too caught up in the system itself. No single system will be perfect. Find the option that works the best for your church, your ministry, and your people, and go with it. Your people are the most important part of check-in, so identify, recruit, train and release your people to go out and make whatever system you're using, in whatever space you have, become the positive environment that demonstrates to everyone an intentional focus worthy of the trust being placed in your kids' ministry.

REFLECTION QUESTIONS

1. Is your check-in more like a monster truck rally or Chuck E. Cheese's? When was the last time you asked an outsider about their check-in experience at your church?
2. How do you train your check-in/check-out teams? Are they prepared to deal with serious emergencies or strange scenarios? Have you empowered them to enforce your own policies, even with the pastoral staff?
3. How well do your emergency policies work? When will you test them?

ABOUT THE AUTHORS

BRENT COLBY

Brent Colby is a Seattle-born coffee drinker who develops leaders in the Northwest Ministry Network and at Northwest University. He wrestles his three kids every day and has an undefeated record up to this point. He has an amazing wife whose nursing degree comes in handy for all of the wrestling injuries. He loves Jesus and loves to talk about leadership and culture at brentcolby.com.

brentcolby.com

LAUREN BEACH

Lauren Beach grew up in the great city of Everett, Washington. She is an orange-loving, beach-going, coffee drinker who is passionate about seeing kids become like Jesus. She graduated from Northwest University with a degree in Pastoral Ministries and an emphasis in Children's Ministry. She is on staff at Faith Assembly of Lacey, and gets to work with some of the greatest leaders around. She is excited for what God is doing in Lacey, Washington.

facebook.com/laurenashleybeach

DAVE M. CAMERON

Dave M. Cameron is the Children's Pastor at Cedar Park Church in Bothell, Washington. He has a loving family that has served the church in a variety of ways. He hides his Canadian accent well and creates some of the most thoughtful and integrated children's programs this side of the border.

facebook.com/dave.cameron.18

CRAIG GEIS

Craig Geis is married to his best friend, has amazing kids, and has a propensity for mixing things up. With a powerfully creative mind and deep empathy for the kids of Spokane, Washington, Craig serves his church with a creativity and energy that is hard to match.

facebook.com/craigeis

DORENE HEETER

Dorene is a veteran children's pastor as well as a gifted mentor and coach. She has served countless men and women as they discover their call to ministry many times over. Missions has always been a driving passion for Dorene and she has participated in several trips to Southeast Asia.

facebook.com/dorene.heeter

SAM KORSLUND

Sam Korslund is an Eastern Washington small town boy at heart who loves to share all kinds of outdoor adventures with his wife and two young boys. Through Kids' Church, coaching and volunteering at school activities, Sam loves to work with kids of all ages to see their lives transformed by the love of Jesus. Sam lives by the ideal of St. Francis of Assisi, who said, "At all times preach the gospel, when necessary use words."

facebook.com/sam.korslund

DAN METTEER

Dan Metteer is a banjo-playing, karaoke-singing children's pastor who loves ultimate frisbee and disc golf. He loves children's ministry because he has a passion to see the next generation take seriously God's call on their lives. He has an exceptionally awesome wife and three above-average kids.

twitter.com/danmetteer

CHANTEL ROHR

Chantel Rohr grew up in Everett, Washington. She attended Northwest University where she met her husband, Brad, and graduated with a BA in Elementary Education. Over the next few years God took her on an unexpected journey as he called her to be a children's pastor. She served on staff at Faith Assembly of Lacey until they were blessed with their first son, David. Now their family lives in Puyallup, WA where they are a part of the Newhope South Hill church plant team and are eagerly awaiting their second son's arrival.

www.facebook.com/bradandchantel.rohr

KATE THAETE

Kate Thaete is the Family Ministries Pastor at Creekside Church in Mountlake Terrace, Washington. She has a passion for kids and a gift for writing. Few leaders share Kate's ability to simplify and express complex ideas in simple ways.

facebook.com/kate.thaete

Joshua R. Zeifle

Joshua R. Ziefle is an Associate Professor at Northwest University and oversees the Youth and Children's Ministries majors. He and his wife Rachel (both New Jersey natives) relocated to the Pacific Northwest in the summer of 2011. For the six years previous to his time at Northwest, Josh served as the youth pastor of Nassau Christian Center in Princeton, NJ. While ministering among the students there, he also completed a PhD in American Church History from Princeton Theological Seminary. He enjoys reading, teaching, and reflecting on topics related to history, practical theology, discipleship, and spiritual formation. He's also a big sci-fi fan. Josh blogs regularly on ministry, culture, history, and other random topics at www.joshuaziefle.net.

twitter.com/jrziefle

NOTES

[1] Daniel J. Levi, *Group Dynamics for Teams* (Thousand Oaks, Calif.: Sage Publishing, 2011), Kindle Edition, p. 83.

[2] Ecclesiastes 4:9–12

[3] Proverbs 21:17

[4] 1 Peter 4:10

[5] Ephesians 4:16

[6] 1 Corinthians 12:27

[7] Stephen Hawking, *A Brief History of Time* (New York: Random House, 1998), Kindle Edition, loc. 2688–2689.

[8] Acts 1:8

[9] You know who you are.

[10] Steven Johnson, *Where Good Ideas Come From* (New York: Riverhead Books, 2010) Kindle Edition, p. 42.

[11] Mortimer J. Adler, Charles Van Doren, *How to Read a Book* (New York: Touchstone, 1972), p. 75.

[12] Psalm 127:3, NIV

[13] Psalm 127:5, NIV

[14] Ephesians 6:1, NIV

[15] Exodus 20:12, NIV

[16] For a brief but by no means exhaustive discussion of these issues, see the following: http://www.christianpost.com/news/youth-ministries-teaching-behavior-modification-not-gospel-73408/ or http://incm.org/how-to-move-from-behavior-modification-to-a-heart-based-approach-in-your-childrens-ministry/.

[17] Proverbs 22:6, NIV

[18] Deuteronomy 6:6–9, NIV

19 I Corinthians 3:1–2, NIV

20 Merriam-Webster Online, accessed 1 November 2014.
http://www.merriam-webster.com/dictionary/ubiquity

21 1 John 2:28–29, NIV

22 Ivy Beckwith, *Formational Children's Ministry* (Grand Rapids, Mich.: Baker, 2010).

23 James Fowler, *Stages of Faith* (New York: HarperOne, 1981). The entire book has insights for readers, but if you are merely interested in the idea of "stages of faith" as such, Part IV is worth its weight in gold.

24 "Original of the Species" by U2, on the album, *How to Dismantle an Atomic Bomb* (2004).

25 Mark 10:13–16, NIV

26 Eugene Peterson, *The Message: The Bible in Contemporary Language*, Mark 10:13–16.

27 George Barna, *Transforming Children into Spiritual Champions* (Ventura, Calif.: Regal, 2003), p. 33.

28 Barna, *Transforming Children*, p. 34.

29 Romans 10:9, NIV

30 John 6:44, NIV

31 Romans 8:34, NIV

32 Lincoln Brewster, "Today is the Day," 2008.

33 Matthew 6:25, 27, 32–33, NASB

34 See Romans 12:1.

35 The Rev. Ron Steinnbrenner introduced me to the nine expressions of worship described in this chapter. I reference him as my source for the aforementioned text.

36 The Hebrew word used here for worship is Shachah, which literally means to bow down in worship. The NASB translates this as worship.

[37] Exodus 33:10 also recounts the story of the Israelites standing to worship God. "When all the people saw the pillar of cloud standing at the entrance of the tent, all the people would arise and worship, each at the entrance of his tent."

[38] Andy Stanley, *Visioneering: God's Blueprint for Developing and Maintaining Vision* (Colorado Springs: Multnomah Books, 1999), p. 17.

[39] Bill Hybels, *Leadership Axioms: Powerful Leadership Proverbs* (Grand Rapids, Mich.: Zondervan, 2012), p. 17.

[40] Hybels, Bill. *Leadership Axioms*, p. 19.

[41] Hybels, p. 18.

[42] Frank E. Gaebelein, David E. Garland, *The Expositor's Bible Commentary, Volume 11* (Grand Rapids, Mich.: Zondervan, 1981).

[43] Andy Stanley, *Deep and Wide: Creating Churches Unchurched People Love to Attend* (Grand Rapids, Mich.: Zondervan, 2012).

[44] "10 of the Most Common Leadership and Management Errors, and What You Can Do to Avoid Them," http://www.mindtools.com/pages/article/leadership-mistakes.htm (accessed October 2014).

[45] Andy Stanley, *Stating Vision Simply* (Leadership Podcast, iTunes).

[46] Stanley, *Stating Vision Simply*.

[47] Stanley, *Stating Vision Simply*.

[48] Andy Stanley, *Next Generation Leader* (New York: Random House, 2006), Kindle Edition, p. 53.

[49] Bhavesh Naik, "Leader vs. Manager: Traits, Qualities and Characteristics," Awayre LLC, http://awayre.hubpages.com/hub/Leader-vs-Manager (accessed October 2014).

[50] John Gilman, "Are You Leading or Managing Your Church?" March 5, 2014, ACS Technologies, http://www.acstechnologies.com/blog/ministry-leadership/leading-managing-church (accessed October 2014).

[51] Warren Bennis, *On Becoming a Leader* (Philadelphia: Perseus Books, 1994).

[52] Chip Heath and Dan Heath, *Decisive: How to Make Better Choices in Life and Work* (New York: Crown Business, 1993), p. 93.

[53] Heath and Heath, p. 95.

[54] Timothy Larsen, "When Did Sunday Schools Start?" Christian History.net, August 28, 2008, http://www.christianitytoday.com/ch/asktheexpert/whendidsundayschoolstart.html (accessed October 2014).

[55] James Fowler, *Stages of Faith: The Psychology of Human Development and the Quest for Meaning* (New York: Harper One, 1995).

[56] Bruce Wilkinson, *The Seven Laws of the Learner: How to Teach Almost Anything to Practically Anyone* (Colorado Springs: Multnomah, 2005).

FUSION CHILDREN'S MINISTRY SERIES

This is Part One of the Fusion Children's Ministry Series. This book is designed to present big ideas about children's ministry relating to theology, leadership, and culture . Learn more about this three-part project and it's big ideas at fusionchildrensministry.com.

THE NORTHWEST MINISTRY NETWORK

The Northwest Ministry Network is a team of churches committed to bring the hope of Jesus to their communities. They minister, as a part of the Assemblies of God, throughout the Pacific Northwest. This book is an expression of the Network's desire to strengthen and develop leaders at home and abroad. To learn more about the Northwest Ministry Network please visit nwministry.com.

60541556R00076

Made in the USA
Lexington, KY
09 February 2017